Battling
the Beast
Within:

---

*Success in Living
With Adversity*

Dedication

*This book is dedicated to the men and women who make up the staff of The Cleveland Clinic Foundation. From transporters and housekeepers to technicians, nurses, and physicians — they all exemplify the **care** in health care. In particular, I want to acknowledge the staff of the Mellen Center for Multiple Sclerosis Treatment and Research, a truly world-class team!*

Thus it is my honor to donate proceeds from this book to the Mellen Center's Patient Education Program.

David T. Williams

Battling the Beast Within

Success in Living with Adversity

by **David T. Williams**

The Cleveland Clinic Press

The Cleveland Clinic Press
9500 Euclid Avenue, NA32
Cleveland, Ohio 44195

Williams, David T., 1949 –

Battling the Beast Within / by David T. Williams

A compilation of vignettes about the author's life, his 28-year
struggle with multiple sclerosis, the people who have and
continue to influence him, and the lessons he has learned about life
from his experiences.

1.) Motivational; 2.) Biographical; 3.) Multiple Sclerosis

Library of Congress Control Number: 2003097087
ISBN 1-59624-001-6

Manufactured in the United States of America

CONTENTS

FOREWORD

As HUMAN BEINGS, most of us are never completely happy and frequently complain about small things. As I approach the age of 63, I look back over my life and remember the challenges of serving in the 60s in Vietnam as a U.S. Marine, an experience from which I returned unscathed. About 24 years ago, I had a cancerous tumor that, while it was a frightening experience, was successfully treated. Surviving both these traumas has made me a better man and, because of them, I am far less likely today to complain about small things. I am truly thankful for this every day.

But it was not until I met David Williams that I really developed a true understanding of courage and why a positive attitude is so important in our lives. If anyone ever had a right to complain it is David – and yet, he does not! For more than 25 years he has been engaged in a constant battle with progressive multiple sclerosis and its related assaults on his spinal cord. He has never let his significant disabilities stop him from effectively carrying out his family and professional responsibilities. In living his life, he is truly an inspiration to everyone who comes in contact with him.

David works hard to make sure that no one feels sorry for him. In fact, his dogged determination to live life to the fullest causes people to look past his disabilities and expect much from him. He makes us forget about his challenges and value his every contribution. It is my hope that some of David's attitudes about life will rub off on you, the readers of this book. If that happens, you will all become better people.

—A. MALACHI MIXON, III
Chairman and CEO
Invacare Corporation

ACKNOWLEDGMENTS

THROUGHOUT THIS BOOK, you will see references to my beloved wife, Fran. As she is in all aspects of my life, Fran has been a collaborator, editor, consultant, partner, and, when necessary, a critic in this book's production. The words "thank you" and "I love you" seem woefully inadequate but, Sweetie, they are all I can offer on this page. Our life together is a living example of those words and their sentiments.

I also want to acknowledge my sons, Eric and Nathan, who have been engaged in my battle with the Beast from the beginning. Throughout this journey, they have always been able to encourage me, involve me in their lives, and believe in me in ways that are indescribable. As boys, they gave me a reason to fight on. As young men, they give me joy and pride in their every accomplishment.

The problem with writing a section like this is that one inevitably leaves someone out who deserves individual mention. I suppose the best protection against hurting the feelings of people who are not listed is to list no one. But I've always been one to throw caution to the wind, so I do want to mention a few people who are special in my life and who have helped influence or assist with the writing of this tome. First is my assistant and friend Vicki Frisbie, who keeps track of me when Fran is not watching. Her friendship and assistance are always invaluable. Next is my boss, Mal Mixon, the chairman and CEO of Invacare Corporation. His ongoing concern and consideration as well as his belief and trust in me for almost 13 years give me the confidence to undertake this endeavor. I also want to acknowledge the friendship and support of friends and colleagues such as Cara Bachenheimer, Hymie Pogir, Mark Sullivan, Julie Jacono, Father Larry Martello, Lena Lindahl, Jack Licate, Bruce Weigl, and

David Miller, who all believed in me enough to be encouraging when I first started thinking about whether I should undertake this project. They also provided invaluable review and critique during the many editorial and review tasks of its production.

I also want to thank, and beg the indulgence of, the numerous philosophers, public figures, poets, and anonymous sources whose words I have used to accentuate certain points in this book. I have chosen not to research and footnote each quote because many of them came to me secondhand through speeches I have heard or articles I have read. If the words are not exact, the sentiment is. Mark Twain once said, **"Good writers often borrow from the works of their contemporaries. Great writers don't borrow, they steal freely."** The jury is out on the quality of my writing, but I will use Mr. Twain's words as justification for the many quotes that appear on these pages, with attribution whenever possible.

INTRODUCTION

WRITING THIS BOOK was an undertaking that took over a year to complete but, in my opinion, was worth the effort for what I got out of the process. It was a cleansing experience that afforded me the opportunity to face the demons that haunt my life and to put my life into perspective.

On these pages you will find frequent and graphic descriptions of the symptoms and casualties of the past 28 years of my life – the period in which I have been engaged in a battle with chronic progressive multiple sclerosis. I did not put this information in this book to evoke pity because, as you will read, I have little use for that emotion. Nor did I share this information to gain your admiration. The information about my disability is there because it provides some insight into how I came to learn the lessons about life expressed on these pages.

Although I have made every effort to be as accurate as possible, I want to acknowledge right up front that much of this book reflects my recollections of things that happened many years ago – things that I, like most people, would rather forget. Some of the memories are so vivid that I am confident of their accuracy. Others are undoubtedly colored by the mind's marvelous ability to block out unpleasant things and rearrange facts in an effort to keep itself from being driven mad. Time and age may also have affected the accuracy of my words.

I am just a regular guy making his way through life while dealing with some fairly significant challenges. People ask me what my secret to success is. The best answer I can give to that question can be found in the words of S.H. Payer, and I recommend them to you as a guide for how to live your life.

Live each day to the fullest.
Get the most from each hour, each day,
and each age of your life.
Then you can look forward with confidence,
and back without regrets.

Be yourself – but be your best self.
Dare to be different and to follow your own star.

And don't be afraid to be happy.
Enjoy what is beautiful.
Love with all your heart and soul.
Believe that those you love, love you.

Forget what you have done for your friends
and remember what they have done for you.

Disregard what the world owes you, and
concentrate on what you owe the world.

When you are faced with a decision,
make that decision as wisely as possible – then forget it.
The moment of absolute certainty never arrives.

And above all else, remember that
God helps those who help themselves.
Act as if everything depended upon you,
and pray as if everything depended upon God.

CHAPTER I

MEET THE BEAST

THE "BEAST" IN THIS BOOK is a nasty disease known as multiple sclerosis or MS. MS affects approximately 2.5 million people worldwide, and each person with MS presents a different set or pattern of symptoms as unique as fingerprints. Further, it is impossible for even the most highly trained clinician to predict either the course or the impact of the disease on an individual's life. Finally, while much progress has been made, the cause of multiple sclerosis is still unknown, and clinicians are therefore limited to managing its symptoms rather than "curing" MS.

Put as simply as possible, multiple sclerosis is an immune disorder that causes the body to attack and destroy the myelin – the insulation that covers nerve fibers – thus short-circuiting or otherwise interrupting the transmission of information within the central nervous system. Over the past 10 years, several new drug therapies have been developed that help reduce the frequency and duration of exacerbations in some forms of MS and the progression of symptoms in the chronic or progressive forms of the disease. Researchers are closer than ever to fully understanding the cause of the disease – the critical first step in developing its cure.

The fact that MS itself is not known to cause premature death is both a blessing and a curse. The curse lies in the fact that, once diagnosed with MS, an individual must learn to live with the fact that without a moment's notice the disease can rear its ugly head and impose new and dramatic changes in his or her life and the lives of family and loved ones. One form of the disease – relapsing/remitting MS – is characterized by periods of exacerbations of symptoms that range from blurred vision and problems with balance all the way to temporary blindness and partial paralysis. Then, as suddenly as they appear, the symptoms are gone and may not reappear for years.

Other forms of the disease are more pernicious. Symptoms appear and never go away or, as is my case, they progress and intensify on an erratic and unpredictable schedule. These forms of MS are called primary progressive, secondary progressive, or chronic progressive MS. My particular version of the disease is chronic progressive MS.

Another of the many idiosyncrasies of MS is that the symptoms and their intensity are directly related to the places within the central nervous system where demyelinization (lesion development) occurs. Lesions in certain parts of the brain can cause significant cognitive problems, speech disorders, and blindness. Lesions in the brain stem and spinal cord affect actions like movement and coordination.

Lesions in the spinal cord have a nasty tendency to cause pain, actually two distinct types of pain. The first is spasticity and its accompanying pain in the muscles and joints. These spasms are caused by erratic signals from the brain or reflex actions that are blocked or scrambled by the lesions. Imagine, if you will, muscles constantly pulling against each other until one weakens and the stronger one knots up into a "charley horse." In their most severe form, these spasms pull on the bones until joints are pressed in unnatural ways and literally grind against each other for hours on end.

Neuropathic pain is another story. Sensory nerves become ultra-sensitive. One contemporary describes it as constantly feeling like someone has sewn sandpaper inside your clothes and used the coarser grades for the areas where the skin is most sensitive (e.g., soles of your feet, fingers and fingertips, and areas that you don't discuss in mixed company). Small scratches hurt like major gashes, and a pimple or a rash can feel like multiple stab wounds.

What these two types of pain have in common is that they intensify exponentially with fatigue in people with MS.

And yet, as bizarre as it may sound, there can be a silver lining to life with the Beast. The very nature of chronic progressive multiple sclerosis is that it presents those who have it with an ever changing array of symptoms, challenges, and opportunities for personal growth. You can allow yourself to become a "victim" of the disease, or you can fight back and, in the process, learn more about yourself and about life than you might learn otherwise. Despite a steady onslaught of new and intense symptoms and challenges, I choose to fight the Beast and in exchange have become its student.

I have been told that all my lesions are in my brain stem and spinal cord. These are the source of intense spasticity and neuropathic pain, the loss of use of my legs and control of my bowels and bladder, and now progressive problems with control of my hands and arms. It has also made fatigue my most mortal enemy.

But, in a way, I'm very lucky. The fact that I am now more than 25 years into the course of the disease with no identifiable lesions in my brain means that it is highly unlikely any will ever develop there. (One of the few times when it is nice to hear somebody say "there is nothing inside your head.") Thus I am spared the symptoms of short-term memory loss, slurred speech, and similar symptoms endured by some of my contemporaries.

About halfway through the process of writing this book, I began to ask myself these questions: Who am I to be giving advice to anyone, and what makes my life worthy of being told on the pages of a book? Like so many questions that have confronted me, the answer came in the form of a political quote, an excerpt from Nelson Mandela's 1994 inaugural address to the people of South Africa.

Our deepest fear is not that we are inadequate. Our deepest fear is that we are powerful beyond measure. It is our light, not our darkness, that most frightens us. We ask ourselves, who am I to be brilliant, gorgeous, talented, and fabulous? Actually who are you not to be all these things? You are a child of God.

Your playing small doesn't serve the world. There's nothing enlightened about shrinking so that other people won't feel insecure around you. We were born to manifest the glory of God that is within us. It's not just in some of us. It's in everyone. And as we let our light shine we unconsciously give other people permission to do the same.

I won't pretend to be glad I have MS or that I would not change things if I could. But in accepting my disease I have been able to open my mind to new ideas and opportunities that have changed me for the better.

One of the struggles that has continued throughout my battle with the Beast has been the fight to remain centered and to remain true to the things that are important to me. I know lots of people with disabilities who are defined by that one aspect of their life. They have surrendered their whole identity to symptoms and limitations imposed by accident or illness. In so doing, they have also surrendered their personality, character, and abilities and have become prisoners within their own bodies, held captive by their diagnostic labels. More significantly, they have turned their backs on many opportunities to learn – to become better people. I will never give in to this.

"He who always gives way to others will end in having no principles of his own." **—AESOP**

The point that Aesop was trying to make is that we all need to know who we are and stand up for what we believe in. Our core beliefs should be regularly tested by exposing them to discussions with those who may not share them. It is not always easy but it is necessary. And in the end, never surrender your identity to anything. Be clear about your own core beliefs and principles and be ready to defend them against all attackers. Giving in to peer pressure is a cop-out. Abandoning who you are because it is convenient is even worse.

This book is my way of sharing my beliefs and principles as well as the lessons I've learned in my battle with the Beast and by being true to myself. It was written to help people deal with life's challenges, whether the source of those challenges is multiple sclerosis or other "tormentors." The lessons that I have learned at the knee of the Beast are really applicable to everyone. We all have our own beasts and demons to face, and perhaps some of what I have learned and experienced can assist others.

What follows is an attempt to tell you what life with the Beast has taught me, how I came to learn these lessons, and how they have affected me. I will also take the liberty of making a few suggestions on how you might apply them to make your life, your relationships, and your business as successful as they can be. I sincerely hope that you find these pages useful, enlightening, and entertaining. Most of all, I hope that some of the words on these pages help the people who read them to conquer the beasts that may challenge them now or in the future.

**"You don't write because you want to say something.
You write because you have something to say."**
—F. SCOTT FITZGERALD

CHAPTER 2

LIFE WITH THE BEAST BEGINS

PERHAPS IT IS THE MYSTERY of it all or maybe even the fear it has brought to my life, but since the beginning I have referred to the disease not by its clinical name but as *the Beast*. Over the years, the Beast has disrupted my family life and visited upon me numerous hospitalizations and several life-threatening situations. It has caused me to change careers more than once, while making constant adjustments in the way I do just about everything. But the Beast has taught me many lessons that I find apply to every aspect of life: business, sports, academics – you name it.

If you asked me what is the one aspect of my disease that frightens me most, I would have to say it is that I'm afraid of falling into the ever-waiting trap of wasting emotional energy wondering, "What's next?" or "Why me?" I've spent too much time in that place already. Writing this book, in part, has helped me face it and move away from it.

As I was about to graduate from high school in 1967, I experienced a sudden and dramatic loss of vision in both eyes. The ophthalmologist thought it was something called optic neuritis that would respond to steroid therapy. He sent me to see a neurologist just to be on the safe side. After more testing, the neurologist agreed and ordered a course of steroid therapy that brought about the desired improvement. During the next eight years, I finished my education, started a career in nuclear medicine, and witnessed the birth of my two sons.

At age 26, I was on the fast track in my chosen career as a nuclear medicine technologist. I was a departmental director in a growing hospital, president of my professional association, and an instructor in a program training new X-ray technologists. I was also very involved in local politics and several community service organizations. Life was good.

Looking back, the course of my disease has run through three phases so far: *what is it*; *you can't do that*; and *let's try this*.

I entered the "what is it" phase in 1975. I began to notice some changes in my peripheral vision. This time the ophthalmologist was a little more concerned, and after a lot of fancy tests sent me off to yet another neurologist. I can remember him saying, "The recurrence of optic neuritis is rare without some more substantial underlying cause such as multiple sclerosis. I want to see you every six months for a while." I never knew two words – multiple sclerosis – could cause such fear and impose such dramatic changes on a person's life.

In late 1976, I began to experience weakness in my right leg with a foot drop that worsened with fatigue. My vision continued to deteriorate to the point that I felt it was now unsafe for me to drive. Now the neurologist got aggressive; CAT scans (MRI was still a research tool), spinal taps, EEG, EMG, and dozens of other tests led to the day in late 1977 when the doctor said, "You most likely have multiple sclerosis, but time will provide the final diagnosis." He tried to soften the blow by telling me that most of the time MS follows a relapsing/remitting course with exacerbation of symptoms followed by periods, up to several years in length, of no symptoms at all. My next major exacerbation occurred less than a year later. Several experts told me at the time that the rapid onset of serious symptoms was unusual, and ever since then the most common word in my medical records has been "atypical."

By 1978, I had entered into the "you can't do that" phase. Well-meaning health care professionals spent a lot of time telling me things like *you can't continue working*, *you can't overextend yourself*, *you can't afford to get too tired*, etc. It seemed as if no one was willing to assess my remaining skills and abilities and help me work out a plan for living with MS. By far, this was the worst phase of my battle with the Beast.

The year 1978 was pivotal in my life. Before it was over, I was no longer able to walk, was declared permanently and totally disabled, and therefore unable to work, and was experiencing severe, seizure-like episodes of spasticity. I was very frightened, felt very alone, and worried constantly about the impact my condition would have on the life of my family. I was especially concerned about my ability to be a good father to my then 7- and 4-year-old sons.

But as is typical in many cases of MS, things settled down and the Beast let me get on with my life, such as it was. The next 20 years were rather unremarkable, at least as far as the progression of my disease was concerned, and I was relatively stable from a neurological point of view.

But the neurology of MS isn't the only aspect of the Beast that I have had to contend with. Several problems have arisen as the result of functional limitations linked to the Beast. For example, the loss of control of my legs left them in a dependent position (constantly sitting), with little or no motion to help move blood around. Over time, I developed blood clots in my legs – a condition known as deep vein thrombophlebitis (the only thing I ever had in common with Richard Nixon). Pieces of clot would break loose, become lodged in my lungs (pulmonary emboli), and pose a significant threat to my life. I was hospitalized three or four times for this problem and eventually had to have surgery to place a filter in the major vein between my legs and my lungs to stop errant clots from killing me. I have been on Coumadin, a blood thinner, ever since.

As I lost control of my legs, I also lost control of my bladder and was very prone to urinary tract infections (UTIs). By 1980, my bladder was so damaged that it was removed and I had to have a urostomy performed to create an outlet for my urine that dumps into an external pouch. The urostomy has had to be revised three times, and I have also had trouble with frequent, severe UTIs and kidney stones that required hospitalization so I could receive massive doses of IV antibiotics.

Nonetheless, this period of neurological stability gave me an opportunity to get on with the business of living. And as everyone knows, "the business of living" is not all peaches and cream. Between 1980 and 1982, I endured some significant professional and personal challenges, not the least of which was the loss of my consulting business and an irreconcilable separation from my wife, which eventually led to our divorce. Still, I was more or less able to keep moving in what felt like a forward direction.

As I will describe later, I returned to work in nuclear medicine for a short time. But in 1982, I began a new career in politics. After actively volunteering in the successful statewide campaign of Ohio Governor Dick Celeste, I was appointed to a senior staff position in his administration, a position I held for eight years. MS remained a big part of my life, but I was able to learn a lot about how government works and how individuals can affect public policy at every level. The experience of working for the governor made the career change from nuclear medicine to politics and public policy an easy one.

When my tenure with the governor ended, my new wife (the beloved Fran) and I started our own business as consultants. We did some work in government relations, worked with a variety of organizations to do strategic planning, helped manage a number of program development projects, and published a small bi-monthly magazine. One of our first clients was Invacare Corporation, the world's leading manufacturer of durable medical equipment. Within two years, Mal Mixon, Invacare's chairman and CEO, asked me to join the firm as the head of its fledgling government relations program. I remain an Invacare employee to this day. During my 11 years with the company, I have developed a reputation in the industry as a leading voice on regulatory and legislative issues that affect the home health care industry.

The past five years have been the worst as far as the progression and intensity of new reminders of the Beast's presence in my life. Whatever stability I had been enjoying began eroding fast, furiously, and with a vengeance. Neither Fran nor I could keep up with the changes, much less figure out how to adjust to them or get ready for the next one. To paraphrase the title of filmmaker Barbara Gordon's biography about her struggle with addiction, we have been *Dancing As Fast As We Can* ever since.

I am now in the "let's try this" phase. Doctors know what is wrong and that the symptoms are real and measurable, but they are not exactly sure what to do to treat the disease or the symptoms. I have endured experimental treatments with a variety of drugs, to no avail. But my health care team is willing to try every option to help me maintain the life I've built for myself. When a new problem pops up, they try to deal with it, leaving no stone unturned.

Doctors now describe my disease as chronic progressive MS and readily acknowledge that they have no clue as to the path it will take, how bad it will get, or what the next "attack" will bring. They only know it will most likely get worse. Pain, spasticity, and weakness in my hands and arms over the past few years have presented even more challenges. Chronic fatigue has been an omnipresent tormentor, but it seems to be playing a bigger role in my life as time goes on.

At this point I need to acknowledge the work of Dr. Jeff Cohen, Dr. Francois Bethoux, two nurse practitioners – Danni Gogol and Kathy Schwetz – and Deb Miller, my case manager/counselor at the Mellen Center for Multiple Sclerosis Treatment and Research of The Cleveland Clinic Foundation.

This team has seen me through some very rough times, aggressively pursued every possible treatment option, and counseled me through the rapid progression of my disease. Their compassion and professionalism are without equal.

The progression of my symptoms continues at a rapid pace. Recently, I have been losing control of my hands and experiencing constant spasticity and neuropathic pain that varies widely in intensity, duration, and location and had been fairly unresponsive to most current therapeutic regimens. Realizing that he had reached the limits of what he could do in dealing with my pain and spasticity, Dr. Cohen referred me to the Pain Management Center at The Cleveland Clinic where Dr. Nagy Mekhail and his nurse assistant, Linda Barker, began to work miracles.

Dr. Mekhail approaches his clinical discipline from the perspective that nobody should have to live with pain. He has been able to build on the work of the Mellen Center staff and implement a protocol that has reduced my spasticity to a manageable level that enables me to remain employed part-time and involved in my community.

What distinguishes the staff of The Cleveland Clinic is that, to a person, they have fully engaged me as an equal partner in planning and executing my own plan of care. They carefully explain the options and the consequences of each option to my wife and me and let us make the decisions on new therapeutic approaches in such a way as to minimize their impact on our lifestyle, albeit with some adjustments.

One of the more notable examples of their thinking ahead with us is this. I have an implanted drug pump that continuously releases morphine and baclofen, a medication to reduce spasticity, directly into my spinal column. One of the advantages of this is that it takes less of the drug to be effective than if I were to take the same medication orally. This is significant because the oral forms of the medication have some nasty side effects, such as constant drowsiness.

It also allows my physicians to combine more than one drug in the mixture, which enables them to help manage more than one symptom at a time, in this case, the pain and the spasticity. However, because my pain and spasticity were so severe, they had to calibrate the dose at a fairly high level.

This meant that I had to take the best part of a full day every three weeks to go into the Clinic to have the pump refilled. And although we have become close as a result of this frequent interaction, Dr. Mekhail was aware of how inconvenient that schedule was. So he initiated a search to find a compounding pharmacy to prepare the medications in a concentration that would require refilling on a less frequent basis. We initially started with six weeks, which seems like a lifetime in between visits, comparatively. Dr. Mekhail's hope is that it will eventually be as long as 12 weeks between refills. I'm sure I'll feel like I have to get reacquainted with him if that happens! But it will be nice. And Fran and I already don't feel as tethered to the hospital as we once did.

Dr. Mekhail and his team are also trying to manage the neuropathic pain in my arms and hands, which is becoming more and more of a problem. They do this with oral medications and take great care to educate me on the implications and side effects of each. With their help, I am able to manage the dosage and the timing in order to minimize the potential negative impact a drug may have on my life and activities. For example, the drugs I take for the pain can also make a person drowsy or affect cognitive abilities like memory, focus, and concentration. One of my clinicians, when I explained that I felt fatigued a good deal of the time, remarked, "Frankly, Dave, I don't know how you even stay awake! The fact that you get up and get things done every day is pretty remarkable in and of itself. Between the disease and the drugs, you need to learn to expect some level of fatigue, my friend." Ultimately, the decision on which drugs to take or, conversely, how much pain I am willing to tolerate is up to me. Dr. Mekhail has given me the knowledge and the tools to make wise decisions in this area.

My life is now a constant three-way struggle among my need and desire to live an active, involved, and productive life, the chronic fatigue that is my most challenging adversary, and the pain that is made worse by that fatigue. The more active I am, the more tired I get. The more tired I get, the more intense my pain and other symptoms become. And the more intense the pain, the harder it is to get the rest I need to remain active – to feel like I am alive and contributing to society.

CHAPTER 3

A DAY IN MY LIFE
WITH THE BEAST

**"Treat people as if they are what they ought to be and
you help them become what they are capable of being."**
—**GOETHE**

IN ORDER TO PROVIDE some perspective on my life and the
opportunities it provides me to learn from the Beast, I
thought it wise to give a quick overview of a typical day in
my life. My disease is progressive and it is important to
understand just what that means on a daily basis. What I can
do for myself is governed by how tired I am. Despite the
many inconveniences of my days, the worst part of each day
is not knowing what the next hour, day, or week will be like.

Six years ago, I dragged myself across the beach on
Martha's Vineyard and played in the waters of the Atlantic
with my nieces. Until three years ago, I was a pretty independent son of a gun and thought nothing of getting up in the
morning, putting in a full day at the office, and then jetting
off to Washington by myself to attend meetings and political
events. For recreation, I would climb onto my handcycle (a
three-wheeled tricycle propelled by a hand crank) and go for
a 30-mile ride. I even completed the annual MS-150 – a two-
day, 150-mile ride to raise money for the National Multiple
Sclerosis Society. Things are much different today.

Now, even the simplest, most routine activity of daily living can be a challenge that requires assistance. For example,
on most days getting out of bed and into my wheelchair
requires two people. The same goes for transferring from the
chair into the shower and back. Buttoning my shirt and
pulling up my pants are also team projects. All this is complicated every third day when I have to insert a suppository

and wait one or two hours for it to work. I'm very envious of my friends who can roll out of bed and be ready to leave for work in 15 minutes.

There have been other seemingly insignificant changes introduced into my daily routine that in reality are not so insignificant. Like most guys, I learned to shave from my father, who used a safety razor (you can't even buy those anymore), a mug with a bar of shaving soap in it, and a brush. Being rebellious, I used shaving lather from a can but stuck to the old handheld razor until a year ago. The increasing weakness and lack of control in my hands has forced me to switch to using an electric razor. The magnitude of this change is akin to sending a baseball pitcher, who has spent his career in the American League with its designated hitter rule, to bat in the 9th inning when his team is behind by a run. We're talking about a major challenge.

Eating required a similar adjustment, although my girth demonstrates that it is one I have managed to work through. I am no longer able to grasp conventional utensils and often rely on Fran to cut things up into bite-size pieces. Some of my favorite foods (rice, homemade soups, and pasta dishes) provide the greatest challenges. When I'm at a restaurant, I look at the menu not only for what sounds tasty but also for what will be the most manageable to eat without embarrassing myself. As I mentioned earlier, fatigue is a huge problem, and I must make a conscious effort to avoid becoming overtired. This is very hard because I have always just kept at things until they were done or until I dropped. There is a significant price to pay if I let that happen now, and the coin of the realm in this arena is pain.

Scheduling and prioritizing my time (never a strong suit) is now an essential part of every day. Before I even get out of bed, I make a mental list of what I must get done, what I'd like to get done, and what I have to accept I won't get done. The toughest list is those things that I must ask someone else to do for me. Then I fit things into a block schedule that allows for three or four hours of activity followed by two or three hours of rest. If I overdo things, fatigue sets in, bringing with it increased pain, reduced control of the fine motor function in my hands, and a weak, raspy voice. Good friends who see me after a good night's sleep often comment that "you look great today" and four hours later will advise me to take it easy because I look like crap!

Pain is a constant companion with the only variable being its intensity. The spasticity in my legs is well controlled and only breaks through when I overextend myself. But my neuropathic pain (Fran and I call it "the bees") is always there. I am a blond with fair skin, so I experienced more than my share of severe sunburn growing up. For me, the best way to describe the pain brought by the Beast is that it feels like a bad sunburn that starts at the soles of my feet and moves up my body to the top of my head. On a scale of one to 10, it can reach 15! It can be so intense that I can hardly stand the weight of my clothes or the brush of a gentle breeze.

I have prescriptions for a cocktail of pain-reducing drugs, but most of the time the best that I can hope for is that they reduce the pain level to a point where I can ignore it. Further, I can't just take a pill if the pain gets bad. Most of the time I have to make a choice between taking medication to relieve the pain and staying alert enough to do my job because almost every drug I take comes with a warning that it may cause drowsiness. The good news is that I have learned that if I keep myself mentally engaged in productive tasks, I am able to ignore the pain to a significant degree. The bad news is that when I do that, the Beast eventually has its way and makes me pay for my indiscretion with even more pain accompanied by absolute exhaustion.

My days end as they begin, with Fran assisting me in getting undressed and into bed – another task that takes time and energy that are not always available at the end of the day. Among the many scars the Beast has left on my body is partial paralysis of my diaphragm and vocal folds, which results in sleep apnea. This means that I frequently stop breathing during the night, which is treated by wearing a mask connected to a machine that forces air into my lungs, reminding me to keep breathing. The good news is that between the machine (known as a continuous positive airway pressure system, or CPAP) and my pain-management cocktail, I sleep pretty well most nights.

"Adversity introduces a man to himself."
—ANONYMOUS

Like most people with chronic conditions, I have good days and bad days, but if I pay attention to things, the good ones outnumber the bad. The hardest thing I have had to adjust to is managing my schedule so that I get enough rest to be alert when I have to be. Setting priorities is difficult because I always thought that I could do everything, and I hate to say "no" to anyone who asks me for help. This is complicated by the fact that my ego has me convinced that there are things that I can do better than anyone else. This inevitably kicks me into the mode of "if you want things done right, do them yourself," and I end up overextending myself. Time management is something I am constantly working to improve.

I know lots of people who say things like "I don't know how you do it. If it were me, I'd just curl up in a ball and die." The truth is that I don't know how I do it either. But I do know that I am driven to keep going by my responsibility to my family, my desire to serve my fellow man, and the love of God. Three pretty powerful forces, wouldn't you say?

So now you have met my Beast and know how it intrudes on my life. However, as bad as it may sound to you, my life is good, and I am happy with what I am able to do and the things that I can accomplish despite the Beast's presence. More importantly, I have learned a lot about living with adversity and how adversity provides great opportunities to become a better person. What follows are some lessons learned battling the Beast that may help you deal with the beasts and demons that all of us encounter as we go through life.

"The best educated human being is the one who understands most about the life in which he has been placed." **—HELEN KELLER**

CHAPTER 4

SELF-PITY IS
A USELESS EMOTION

ONE OF MY HOBBIES is nature photography. I've always had bad vision, and I've found that the camera's lens can compensate for this deficit. In late 1977, I took my camera and found myself by a small stream that was framed by pines and still flowing briskly despite the freezing cold and fresh snow on the ground. I took a photo of this scene. It hangs on my wall to this day as a reminder of my last solo trip into the forest. Within a year of that trek, the Beast had robbed me of my ability to walk.

It wasn't long after that walk in the woods that I climbed a ladder to break up some icicles on the edge of our home's roof. The roof was not a high one, and I was only a few steps up on the ladder. But my legs became wobbly on me without notice (a phenomenon I was still trying to ignore) and I fell off the ladder. Although I didn't have far to fall, I did bang myself up pretty badly. I managed to get myself into the house and lay down. It was late in the day, and, as it happened, I fell asleep for the night. When I woke in the morning, I couldn't move anything below my waist.

The doctors who treated me at the time assumed it was another progression of MS. We'll never know for sure. I went through six months of physical therapy and was learning to walk with braces and forearm crutches. (Talk about looking and feeling like a robot!) After several hospitalizations in acute care settings, I was told that I would have to use a wheelchair full time and was transferred to a rehab facility to learn to deal with life from a seated position. By the time I was discharged from rehab, the decision was made that I qualified for permanent and total disability benefits. My job as the Director of Nuclear Medicine, Ultrasound, and Radiation Safety at a local hospital was gone, and I was instructed to go home and enjoy retirement. I was 29 years old!

After leaving the rehab hospital, I had nothing to do but think about what I had lost. I rarely thought about the future, and when I did I became despondent about how bleak it looked. I got so low that I contemplated taking my own life. The thought of leaving my sons fatherless and the recognition that suicide was the coward's way out kept me going.

As you might expect, I went through life in a huge blue funk. I thought "Why me?" and spent most of the time and all my emotional energy feeling sorry for myself. Friends tried to cheer me up and made every effort to keep me involved, but the awkwardness of my new circumstances and the pain of feeling "different" were emotionally paralyzing – far more paralyzing than the paralysis that put me in a wheelchair. Then one of life's ironies kicked me in the head and made me realize that focusing on the negative was not doing me, or anyone around me, any good.

Self-pity can be overwhelming if you let it. If you dwell on the idea that you are defeated, you are. If you let yourself believe your life is over, it is. And if you accept the idea that you are incapable of being a productive member of society, you will be. The worst aspect of self-pity is that there is no cure unless you want one. There are no drugs, counselors, or treatments that can "cure" a case of self-pity. But if you leave yourself open to the idea, life can present you with opportunities to escape the bonds of self-pity.

My awakening evolved from the fact that I am, as they say, a political junkie. I never miss the news. I believe that CNN and C-SPAN are the two greatest inventions of the 20th century. I have an insatiable appetite for American history, political biographies, and books on political strategy. One of my life heroes, Senator Hubert H. Humphrey, died a few months after I was discharged from the rehab hospital. The tribute in the local newspaper was a marvelous portrait of this man who was known as "The Happy Warrior." The portrait included this quotation, excerpted from an interview he gave as he was battling the cancer that eventually took his life:

> **"When I start feeling sorry for myself, I tell myself . . . we can't do anything about it so just get on with the business of living. If we don't overcome self-pity, the game is all over. . . . The biggest mistake people make is giving up."** —HUBERT H. HUMPHREY

Knowing my respect and admiration for Senator Humphrey, a couple of friends – Bob and Margaret Schubring – had the tribute framed for me. It, too, hangs on my office wall. It was the kind of thoughtful gesture that friends do for each other, but I doubt that they know how profoundly their gift changed my life.

Those words serve as a constant reminder that feeling sorry for myself was wasting precious time and energy and keeping me from finding ways to conquer the new challenges that I was facing. They helped me see that my life was not over and that self-pity was keeping me from seeing the new opportunities that now lay before me. As if he were standing by my side, Senator Humphrey challenged me to reassess my life, inventory my skills and abilities, and figure out how I could use them to regain my status as a productive member of society.

While the Beast gave me my particular case of self-pity, anyone can be challenged by a set of circumstances that has them asking, "*Why me?*" Failed relationships, job problems, business losses, or just plain old bad luck can quickly evolve into self-pity. I'm not a Pollyanna and I know that a certain amount of self-pity is a natural part of life. But you can't allow these feelings to take over your every thought and action.

A certain amount of grieving is OK – even necessary sometimes. Still, you must begin to look for ways to deal with things as quickly as possible. When you are feeling low, look for something or someone who can take your mind off your problems. If your challenge is life-altering, take the time to reassess your life and your priorities and see what your options are. If necessary, look for a new path and see where it takes you. Whatever you do, keep moving forward because that is what will keep you alive.

CHAPTER 5

ANGER BREEDS ISOLATION AND LONELINESS

THROUGHOUT MY 28-YEAR battle with the Beast, I have, on many occasions, been angry at the seemingly endless string of challenges that have been placed before me.

Throughout the early years of the struggle, I was very much an "angry young man." A large part of this stemmed from the fact that many of the health care professionals I was dealing with at the time spent a lot of time telling me what I could not do and that I should just accept the consequences of my diagnosis. The pictures they would paint of my future were dark and hopeless. As a result, I would blow up at the least little provocation.

The fact that I could no longer drive and used a wheelchair for mobility meant that I had to rely on public transportation to get around the community. At that time, most transit systems did not have lift-equipped buses and used small vans to meet the needs of people with disabilities. This type of door-to-door service is called paratransit. It was a demeaning reminder of the loss of a great deal of my personal independence and the fact that I was somehow transformed into a person who needed "special" services because of my disability.

So, if the paratransit bus was late, I called the bus company and yelled at the operator. Some political acquaintances were subjected to my constant ranting about how screwed up the system was and got even with me by appointing me to the transit system's advisory board. I soon learned that the bus was late because the demand for service far outstripped the available resources. That poor operator I was constantly yelling at had no control over the situation. The good news is that my being a member of the advisory board helped improve the quality of service for me. However, it took another decade and the passage of the Americans with Disabilities Act for the changes in the system to materialize that would make public transportation fully accessible to all people with disabilities.

I would also get angry over such things as the placement of the furniture in a friend's home that was not conducive to wheelchair access. I would lose control and accuse them of being ignorant and insensitive. In an effort to assert my independence, I would be rude to people who would hold a door for me by saying something like "*I can take care of that myself*" rather than a more appropriate "*Thank you.*" At times it seemed like my anger knew no bounds and the targets of my anger included family, friends, and strangers. I was not a fun guy to be around.

> **"Anger is the most impotent of passions. It effects nothing it goes about, and hurts the one who is possessed by it more than the one against whom it is directed."** —CARL SANDBURG

In short order, some of my friends stopped including me in activities. Friction erupted within my family, and my sons began keeping their distance when Dad was having a bad day. My anger undoubtedly contributed to the eventual demise of my first marriage. Sometimes you have to hit rock bottom before you realize that something has to change.

In time, I came to realize that nobody I knew was intentionally rearranging furniture to create wheelchair obstacle courses (although I still have a few friends who get a kick out of placing things as close together as they can just to test my driving skills). Like me, they were adjusting to my disability.

I thank God every day that my sons, Eric and Nathan, demonstrated patience and maturity beyond their years.

They stuck with me and helped me see how my anger was hurting other people. The look in their eyes showed me the pain and embarrassment my temper visited upon others. Well before either of them had reached their tenth birthday, they had taught me that uncontrolled anger was a one-way ticket to a life of loneliness and isolation.

A basketball covered with the scribbled signatures of a dozen 10-year-old boys is a reminder of how Eric helped me deal with the Beast. He had signed up to play basketball in a church league. When he was told that there were not enough coaches for all the teams, he told the group that "my dad knows a lot about basketball, maybe he can be our coach." We ended the season with a record of seven wins and four losses, but the experience of being responsible for the team and being a role model for sportsmanship was an enormous help in my effort to get control of my temper.

More importantly, Eric was the first person to look beyond my disability and find a way to use my talent, knowledge, and ability. It was not easy because most of the gyms had steps and, as I would later learn, the game is different from a wheelchair. But Eric gave me the gift of being his dad, his coach, and the coach of the St. Therese Wildcats! As I mentioned, we did not have a great record, but the season was a huge step in the process of learning to live my life with the Beast and to control my temper.

It is often said that some people just can't control their temper. Bunk! Learning to control anger is difficult and sometimes even requires professional intervention. The first step is realizing that your anger hurts other people. The next is that you, and you alone, must be the one who decides that you must get control of your anger.

"Anger kills both laughter and joy. What greater foe is there than anger?"

—TIRUVALLUVAR, Tamil sage and poet

It is no secret that we build our relationships with the people who make us happy and avoid people who are incapable of laughter and joy.

Everyone needs to let off a little steam now and again, but we also need to control these outbursts and take great care to ensure that we don't hurt anyone else in the process. Oddly enough, the big things do not seem to bother me as much as the little ones do. The appearance of a new symptom does not bother me as much as finding out that I can't get into the bathroom of a new restaurant because the door is too narrow. Being unable to drive a car any longer is dwarfed by seeing a car parked illegally in a parking space reserved for people with disabilities.

> **"Those who control their anger have great understanding; those with a hasty temper will make mistakes."** —SOLOMON
> **Proverbs 14:29**

Moreover, I've found the truth in the old saying that you can attract more bees with honey than with vinegar. Yelling at the restaurant's owner will not make the bathroom door any wider. Having a conversation, however, helps him understand why fixing the situation would be good for business and can yield positive results. Anger closes the door on this kind of dialogue; it precludes finding solutions to solvable problems.

I still get mad at obstacles that the Beast puts in my way. But I've reached the point that the only person I yell at is myself, and I am working on that behavior all the time. This is not to say that I don't enjoy a good argument every once in a while, especially if the argument is about a topic I care about. The key is to say my piece, listen to the other side of the issue, and move on.

"In seeking the truth you have to get both sides of the story." **—WALTER CRONKITE**

No matter how violently I may disagree with someone, I try to end the discussion in a civil manner. This is not always easy and sometimes seems downright impossible, but just trying reduces both anger and its associated stress.

When I was a young boy, my grandmother could tell when I was getting angry and would order me to sit down and slowly count to 10 before saying anything that I might later regret. It was good advice then and remains so today.

"When angry, count to ten before you speak; if very angry, count to a hundred!" **—PRESIDENT THOMAS JEFFERSON**

CHAPTER 6

IDENTIFY AND EMULATE
LIFE HEROES

I HAVE YET TO SEE a book that is written about "life heroes." My definition of a life hero is a person who sets an example that, if emulated, can make you a better person. Some life heroes are famous not for their heroic acts, but for the way they live their lives. When looking for your own heroes, look first for the great traits in common people rather than the common traits in great ones. You will find life heroes in the most unlikely places. In fact, the person sitting next to you at any moment may just turn out to be a hero worth emulating.

I can distinctly remember how frightened and alone I felt when I was in the intensive care unit of our local hospital in July of 1978. A reaction to new medications had caused a severe exacerbation of symptoms that included a series of "seizures" that left me unable to move anything. A tube was inserted in my throat because I had stopped breathing a couple of times, and I could not talk. The whole experience taught me what it must feel like to be buried alive.

I lay there acutely aware of everything that was going on around me and everything that was said about me. To this day, I remember the smell of the antiseptic soaps used to clean the room, the pace of the steady drip of my IV, and the "whiz and pop" sound of the ventilator that was breathing for me. Fighting to stave off unconsciousness, I stared at the ceiling tiles and tried to count the dots, comparing one tile to the next to see if there were a pre-established pattern (my physics training convinced me that a random pattern was impossible to achieve). I even remember thinking how butt ugly the color of the curtains that surrounded my bed was and wanting to tell someone to change them to something less somber and depressing.

My most vivid memory of that experience is that I can still hear the voice in my head screaming, "*No! You're wrong!*" as a new intern, standing close enough that I could hear his every word, told my family to prepare themselves because I might not make it until the next morning. As someone who had worked in a hospital most of my adult life, I remember thinking that the worst time to be in the hospital is during the month of July because that is when the new interns and residents arrive.

Then a hero arrived in the form of a neurologist by the name of Dr. John Gardner, a short balding man with silver hair and horn-rimmed glasses. His most memorable features were a cherubic smile and a voice that never conveyed worry or fear. While efficient, he never seemed hurried and had an air of competence that was comforting. In the physician's dictionary of important characteristics, his picture should accompany the concept of correct bedside manner.

After a quick review of my chart and a cursory exam, Dr. Gardner realized that I was aware of what was going on and very frightened. He grabbed my hand firmly and said these words, which I will never forget: "We've got ourselves into quite a mess here, Dave, and you have to help us turn things around. It's going to be quite a fight, but we can do this if you pitch in." Then in a kind and gentle voice he reminded me that my sons needed me.

Dr. Gardner gave me three things that the scores of other professionals involved in my care up to that time had not. First, he gave me confidence that I could survive. Next, he gave me a reason to want to fight back against whatever was attacking my body. Finally, he made me aware of the fact that I was in control of my own destiny, a partner in whatever was going to happen to me from that moment on.

Most people would label Dr. Gardner as a good physician

with exceptional communication skills. To me he is a hero. His gentle demeanor, calming voice, and palpable confidence led me through one of my darkest hours. He taught me that I had to be the leader of my own health care team if we were to prevail in my battle with the Beast – a lesson that I take seriously to this very day.

"Love of glory can only create a great hero; contempt of glory creates a great man." —C.M. DE TALLEYRAND

Over the years I have learned that heroism lies not in the size of the accomplishment but in the passion and commitment with which it is pursued. Former Senator Max Cleland (D-GA) personifies the truth of this statement. I am honored to be able to call him a close friend of more than 20 years. He is one of my life heroes and would be a good one for anyone involved in any service arena.

Max left both legs and one arm on the battlefields of Vietnam. After a long and arduous period of rehabilitation, Max responded to yet another call to public service. Despite the challenges imposed by his disabilities, he ran for and was elected to the Georgia State Senate. When Jimmy Carter was elected president, he asked Max to serve as the Administrator of the Veterans Administration – the first disabled Vietnam veteran to hold this post. After that, he was elected Georgia's Secretary of State and, in 1996, was elected to the United States Senate. He lost his bid for reelection in 2002. His opponent and his manager ran a campaign that accused Senator Cleland of being unpatriotic. This from men who had never been in the military or served a minute in harm's way.

Max likes politics, but he loves public service. He enjoyed a reputation as one of the hardest working members of Congress and always found the time to maintain personal contact with constituents. I have seen him work a crowd, and each person he talked with, although it may have been for only a minute or two, was left with the indelible impression that he or she was the most important person in the room. Moreover, he is a man of honor. Political expedience has always been subordinate to what he believes to be right, and he works hard to understand all sides of every issue before taking a position.

"The acts and accomplishments of common people are the punctuation marks for the words and wisdom of great ones." —MAX CLELAND

One of my first political battles after the Beast forced me to live my life in a seated position was the fight to get the Cleveland public transit system to become accessible to customers with disabilities. That effort eventually led to helping get the Americans with Disabilities Act (ADA) passed and signed into law. Senators Ted Kennedy (D-MA), Bob Dole (R-KS), and Tom Harkin (D-IA) were vocal advocates. There were many supporters in the House of Representatives, but I believe that it was the passion for justice shared by then Speaker Tom Foley (D-WA) and Minority Leader Bob Michael (R-IL), coupled with the leadership of President George Herbert Walker Bush, that got this landmark civil rights legislation enacted in 1990. President Bush, Senator Dole, and Representative Michael are great men who bucked the conservatives within the Republican Party and did a wonderful thing for millions of Americans. I should note that I am proud to call myself a lifelong, partisan Democrat, and I am proud that these men acted not as partisan politicians, but as public servants in the course of doing what is right for the greater good of all Americans. I try to incorporate a little of their passion and motivation into my own performance as a member of the city council in my hometown of Amherst, Ohio.

I'm guessing that some of this philosophy must be working because people I don't know stop me on the street to compliment me on my performance on council. As often as not, these people will say something like, "I don't know how you can put up with all of that. I know I couldn't do it." If Fran is with me, she will jump right into the conversation and say, "Because until we have a bloody coup in Washington, this is the only system we have. Somebody has to do it and I want to make sure it's the good guys." (Did I mention that Fran is one of my biggest supporters and the treasurer of my campaign committee?) I really love public service, and I'm glad that at least one of my constituents considers me to be one of the good guys.

Bob Lynch is another hero. A fall while rock climbing at age 19 left Bob with high-level quadriplegia and forced him to redirect his career plans from engineering to law. In his law practice, Bob specializes in representing people with disabilities whose rights, as defined in the ADA and elsewhere, have been violated. Many of his clients do not have the ability to pay his usual fees, but he nonetheless provides them zealous representation and has made the promise of the ADA come alive for dozens of people. His work and his words punctuate the actions of the men who wrote and passed the ADA.

I like to think of my life as an unfinished mosaic, the pieces of which are provided by the dozens of people who I consider to be my heroes. Dr. Gardner taught me compassion and the ability to overcome any obstacle the Beast may put in my path. Max Cleland is a role model I emulate as a member of our city council and in my various political activities. Bob Lynch's work reminds me how much can be accomplished by people who don't seek credit or adulation.

"It's amazing what we can accomplish when nobody takes the credit." —PRESIDENT HARRY S. TRUMAN

Lots of people might write this off as sucking up, but my boss, Mal Mixon, is one of my life heroes. We have an interesting relationship based on challenging each other on issues and politics to the point of occasional shouting matches. Sometimes Mal tries to blame me when someone in "the government" passes a law or promulgates a rule that displeases him. Because Mal is a dyed-in-the-wool Republican, I get it with both barrels if the root of his anger happens to be a member of the Democratic Party. I have learned to accept being the target of these occasional assaults as one of the essential functions of my job because once he has vented his frustrations it is back to business as usual. And as in any employer/employee relationship, we have our areas of disagreement and even occasionally accuse each other of being full of it (he tells me I'm full of it, but I don't articulate the words – not out of fear, but out of respect for him).

What makes Mal my hero is his loyalty to friends and associates. He will tell you that his loyalty comes from the lessons he learned while serving in the Marine Corps during the Vietnam War. But it is much more than that. Mal really cares about people, and if he believes that you are doing your best, he will go to the ends of the earth to make you feel appreciated.

As the Beast has progressively limited my physical abilities, Mal has been the first one in line to help me figure out a way to accommodate the changes imposed by my disability. Many employers would look for a way to remove someone like me from my position and fill it with a person who presents no challenges or requires no accommodations. Not Mal. Through his acts he has taught me about loyalty, and because of this he is one of my heroes.

"Lack of loyalty is one of the major causes of failure in every walk of life." **—NAPOLEON HILL**

One of the things that keeps me going is the search for more people who can enrich my life – who can be added to my list of life heroes. This search has opened my eyes and my mind to people I might otherwise have avoided and has added many people to the growing list of friends who make my life enjoyable. Anyone who is open to meeting new people and identifying new life heroes is simultaneously giving themselves new opportunities for personal growth.

CHAPTER 7

A SETBACK IS A SETUP FOR A COMEBACK

EVERY ASPECT OF HUMAN existence carries with it the inevitability of occasional setbacks. However, a bright future awaits those of us who see each setback as an opportunity to make a comeback – to build on our failures, mistakes, or misfortunes to achieve even greater things.

Three years ago, I was at the top of my game again. I was a key executive at Invacare; an acknowledged expert on health care policy; a much sought-after speaker for a variety of local, state, and national events; and the first executive director of the national association representing rehab technology providers. I was making bi-weekly trips to Washington, had speaking engagements all over the country, and was serving my first term as a member of Amherst City Council. The more challenging the assignment, the better I liked it.

The Beast, it seems, became jealous of my success and decided it was time to force me to reassess my priorities – again. It was then that the Beast added chronic fatigue, intractable pain and weakness, and progressive loss of control in my arms and hands to my menu of symptoms. The more tired I got, the more intense these symptoms became. My health care team advised me that it was time to cut back, to reduce my schedule, and to avoid stress. There were even suggestions that I might want to consider early retirement on a disability pension. Without a doubt, this setback has been the greatest challenge so far in my battle with the Beast.

At first I refused to acknowledge the setback and figured if I ignored it long enough it would go away. It soon became obvious that this was a bad strategy. Then I started making deals with myself – I'll cut back a little here so that I can continue to give 100% there – with the idea being that I could somehow keep the old package intact. The problem was that I ended up shortchanging everyone, most importantly myself and my family.

I soon came to realize that if I remained open to new ideas – Fran and I call it *the new package* – I could once again vanquish my tormentor.

> **"Yes, we can have pessimism of the intellect but that must be offset with an optimism of the will."**
> **—ANTONIO BORNSCI**

The first decision was that early retirement was not an option for a variety of reasons. So Fran, my boss, and I set about the task of determining what I could continue to do, what could get done by someone else, and how I could continue to be fair to my family, my employer, and myself. This process reminded me that the Beast was not only my tormentor but an enemy of my family, my friends, and my employer.

One of the first things we realized had to be cut back was the extensive travel because it exhausted me and intensified my other symptoms. A competent young woman was hired to fill the trade association job, which allowed me to reduce my trips to Washington from 31 in 1999 to 12 in 2002.

Washington is a place where you have to be seen on a regular basis to be relevant, so it remains important for me to make the rounds on Capitol Hill as often as possible. I used to accomplish this by taking the first morning flight to Washington, cramming 10, 15, or 20 appointments into one or two long days, and returning home on the last flight out. I now spend four or five days in Washington at a time, which allows me to build in time for rest each day. Invacare also generously pays for Fran to travel with me and help with the many activities of daily living that I can no longer manage on my own, tasks that can be very frustrating and often contribute to my fatigue.

To put it frankly, I really enjoy the spotlight. One friend refers to me as an "elder statesman" of the industry – a role I thoroughly enjoy. I was frequently invited to make a speech or presentation to the many different industry groups, and I always accepted. I have had to become much more selective in accepting these invitations because I just don't have enough energy to do them all. Air travel for all Americans has changed dramatically since September 11, 2001, and air travel for people who use wheelchairs is no exception. Even before 9/11, flying with a wheelchair was full of inconveniences and physical demands. These have been brought to higher levels with the new security measures. So for reasons inherent in my own physical needs and those introduced because of the security changes, I have also had to become selective about air travel. But an opportunity to continue to share my thoughts and opinions in a different manner soon revealed itself.

I now write articles and commentaries for several trade publications and have become a "reliable source" for reporters covering the home medical equipment (HME) service industry. Hardly a month goes by that you don't see my byline in several publications. Best of all, one publication has set aside the back page of each issue for a commentary co-written by Cara Bachenheimer, a colleague at Invacare, and me. Like George Will and Meg Greenfield in *Newsweek*, we work hard to make these short commentaries thought-provoking and a little controversial. It's a great gig!

> **"Luck is a matter of preparation meeting opportunity."**
> **—OPRAH WINFREY**

Another piece of the "new package" provided by my employer is that I have been able to modify my schedule to reduced, more flexible hours. Invacare also outfitted a complete office in my home, eliminating the need to travel back and forth to our corporate headquarters and enabling me to rest when I need to. This makes it possible for me to remain a member of the Invacare team – a gift of incalculable value.

The new package also enables me to remain active in politics and my community, and to spend more quality time with Fran and our friends. I have even developed hobbies that help reduce the stress – water gardening, raising ornamental koi and other fish, and photography.

> **"He who has a why to live for can bear almost any how."** —**FRIEDRICH NIETZSCHE**

This comeback felt complete; however, the Beast was gearing up to deliver another devastating blow. But I can face that because I know that I can make the necessary adjustments. The key will be to avoid fixating on the negative things that caused the setback and see how minor adjustments in my priorities can lead to another comeback.

We are each personally responsible for everything that is done to us or for us. As difficult as it is to accept this, doing so allows you to grow. That is what a comeback is – personal growth based on a bad or unpleasant experience.

It's foolish to spend time and energy looking for someone to blame when you experience a setback because time spent this way is time spent standing still. The best thing about a comeback is that it is something that you make happen for yourself. Take pride in that fact. Accepting responsibility for the good things in your life is enriching and yet another catalyst for personal growth.

> **"A man can fail many times but he isn't a failure until he begins to blame somebody else."** —**JOHN BURROUGHS**

CHAPTER 8

WORDS DRIVE THOUGHT, THOUGHT DRIVES ACTION

As THE VISIBLE IMPACT of the Beast's attacks upon my body increased, I became more acutely aware of how inadvertently hurtful language can be. Friends and family members used terms like "crippled," "confined to a wheelchair," and "victim" to describe me. While rooted in ignorance and not spoken in malice, it was nonetheless very painful to hear myself referred to in this way. The good news is that this experience has made me very sensitive to the way we all refer to people who are different from us.

People of African descent have matriculated through dozens of derogatory terms as they have fought for their own equality and civil rights. Negroes became blacks; blacks became Afro-Americans. The current "politically correct" terms most commonly heard are African American and "people of color." As I became more involved in the political life of the disability community, I became aware of a similar phenomenon, which was amplified as I became an activist pushing for the passage of the Americans with Disabilities Act. I began to see the parallels between our struggle and those of other minorities seeking their civil rights and realized that the first step towards equality was to be recognized as people first.

"Words are the most powerful drug used by mankind."
—RUDYARD KIPLING

This was an eye-opening experience for a guy who frequently referred to his adversaries as "retards" when he was a kid. In those days, that was the lowest verbal blow you could land. Looking back, I can remember one boy who flew into a rage whenever he would be so labeled. I now know why. His older brother was diagnosed with Down's syndrome, a form of mental retardation, and my verbal assault on him was also an assault on his brother. Like most kids, I could be a real insensitive jerk.

Now the tables were turned, and the negative connotations of "cripple" and "victim" were my burden to bear. I wanted to be recognized for who I was, what I had accomplished, and what I could do. I wanted to be known as Dave, Dad, a professional, a politician – anything other than a cripple or a victim. Then I read an article by Mary Johnson about a concept referred to as "people first language." Mary was the publisher of a radical, underground newspaper by and for people with disabilities known as the *Disability Rag*.

"All words are pegs to hang ideas on."
—HENRY WARD BEECHER

The concept was elegant in its simplicity, but I knew it would be challenging to implement. The object was to preface any phrase involving disability with either "person" or "people" so that the focus would be on the humanity of the individual and not the generally negative perceptions associated with disability. The idea was formed and spread by a few grown folks who happened to have mental retardation. They were tired of always being referred to as "the retarded." They weren't particularly wild about the term "developmentally disabled" either, which was the term that emerged in the late 70s and early 80s. They simply wanted to be referred to, described, thought of, and treated as *people*. Oh, and if folks needed more descriptions, *people with mental retardation* would be OK. I became an instant convert. After all, it was much better to be referred to as a person with MS than a victim of the disease. Like many converts, I began preaching the gospel of "people first" language with the fervor of a crusader.

"A word is dead when it is said, some say. I say it just begins to live that day." —EMILY DICKINSON

I volunteered in Dick Celeste's 1982 campaign for governor of Ohio. During the course of the campaign, Dick demonstrated a unique sensitivity to and understanding of the state's responsibility to include people with disabilities in all its programs and activities. One way he "walked the talk" was to insist that a sign-language interpreter be present at all his public appearances – a practice he continued throughout his two terms as governor. Dick was the first major politician in America to use interpreters, a practice now imitated by others who may not understand that there is more to disability awareness than American Sign Language.

During one of his campaign staff meetings, Dick announced that he wanted the voters to know that he would establish a position, reporting directly to him, to review and revise programs for people with disabilities as necessary. I know him well enough to say that this came from his heart, but I'm also savvy enough to see that it was a very strategic political move. When you add together the number of people with disabilities in Ohio with their family and friends, you have a significant block of voters who had a reason to vote for the first candidate to publicly articulate his knowledge of and support for the issues important to them.

Dick won the election, and after a few months I wrote him to remind him of his promise to appoint an advocate to his senior staff. I still remember the evening when the phone rang and Eric, then 11, answered it. Without covering the mouthpiece he turned and yelled, "Dad, it's some guy who says he is the governor."

I took the call and sure enough it was Governor Celeste

on the line. Dick said, "I have your letter but can't seem to find your resume or application. Can you meet me in Columbus on Friday?" A week later (I had to be checked out by his security staff) Governor Celeste appointed me to be the first director of the Governor's Office of Advocacy and that ended my tenure as a permanently and totally disabled person who was unable to work.

The appointment was an opportunity to "change the world" – it presented itself for me to expand my crusade, and I took every advantage of it. The People First Initiative started with the drafting of executive orders mandating the use of "people first" language in all official publications produced by the State of Ohio and renaming state panels and functions to reflect the "people first" concepts. As soon as the governor signed the document, the Governor's Council on Disabled Persons became the Governor's Council on People with Disabilities. Within months, other states were following suit. The movement grew, and soon the President's Committee on Employment of the Handicapped became the President's Committee on the Employment of People with Disabilities. I certainly don't claim sole credit for these accomplishments, but with Governor Celeste's encouragement and support, I was fortunate enough to play a significant role in making it happen in Ohio. In turn, he shared his actions with his fellow governors, and the rest, as they say, is history.

The change in names was much more than symbolic. People in government began to see their clients and constituents as people – people who had dreams, abilities, and interests and not just a variety of clinical diagnoses. Rather than performing tests and evaluations to see what their clients could not do, vocational rehab counselors began the intake process by talking with their customers about what they wanted to do. Barriers to full participation in the lives of their community slowly began to be eliminated.

The concept of "people first" language requires some discipline. Sometimes, the task is made more difficult when people who are different from you use what could be considered derogatory words and phrases among themselves. For example, whenever a group of guys who use wheelchairs gather together it is inevitable that one or more of them will use the word "gimp." Ignore that. It is harmless banter among friends and is restricted to use by members of the "tribe." Instead, adhere to this simple rule and you will soon be conversant in "people first" language: never refer to anyone else in terms that you would not want to have used to describe yourself.

"There are no secrets to success. It is the result of preparation, hard work and learning from your failures."
—COLIN L. POWELL

Emboldened by the success of Ohio's People First Initiative, the governor asked me to get more involved in the national effort to get a law passed defining the civil rights of people with disabilities. The first draft of the legislation was called the Disability Rights Act of 1986 and received little attention and few supporters. It died in committee. But words are powerful things.

Thanks to the governor, I was appointed to a group known as the Congressional Advisory Council on the Rights and Empowerment of People with Disabilities. The council rolled out a new draft of the Disability Rights Act in 1988, and this time it was called the Americans with Disabilities Act. The legislation was introduced in 1989 with over 120 co-sponsors and was passed in 1990 by overwhelming majorities in both the House and the Senate. Minor changes in the legislative intent and the careful selection of the words used in the title transformed the effort from doing something symbolic for "the disabled" to passing the first comprehensive legislation defining – and protecting – the civil rights of *Americans* with disabilities.

"People first" language is just one example of how words drive thought and thought drives action. The idea is applicable to every aspect of life.

If you say that a task is impossible, it will be. If you say there is no hope, there probably isn't any. If you come in to work in the morning and say that you are having a bad day, you will have a bad day. On the other hand, if you say a task is challenging, you will be challenged to try it. My grade school teachers often admonished me to choose my words wisely. Now I know better than ever what these teachers meant.

"Words once spoken can never be recalled."
—WENTWORTH DILLON

We often put ourselves at a mental disadvantage by not thinking before we speak. More importantly, it is so easy to cause another person unnecessary pain or anguish by using terms that they find offensive. I know that some folks try to rationalize a poor choice of words by saying that they grew up using words like "cripple," "nigger," "retard," or "towelhead" to refer to people who were different from themselves. That's a lousy excuse. Anyone who wants to purge their speech of such words and phrases can if they really want to.

The use of negative or pejorative terms to refer to another person results in low expectations of that individual, poor communication with that person, and a failure on your part to acknowledge that you are speaking about another human being. Words do drive thought and thought does drive action.

"You have to expect things of yourself before you can do them."
—MICHAEL JORDAN

CHAPTER 9

GIVE YOUR LOVE FREELY

"Love alone is capable of uniting living beings in such a way as to complete and fulfill them, for it alone takes them and joins them by what is deepest within themselves."
                                        —PIERRE DE CHARDIN

IN A TIME OF PERSONAL CRISIS, there is nothing as comforting as the touch of someone who loves you. Over the past 28 years, the Beast has presented dozens of frightening challenges: numerous surgeries to deal with a non-functioning bladder, raging infections, blood clots in my lungs, uncontrollable seizure-like episodes, and intense, intractable pain. It would be easy to feel very alone and vulnerable at these times, but I have been blessed by the love of my wife and my sons. Just knowing that they were there has eased many otherwise unbearable burdens.

One incident stands out among many. A surgical mishap in 1995 resulted in a serious infection with sky-high fevers that sparked intense, painful spasms that racked all my extremities. The fevers and the high doses of antibiotics caused hallucinations (I swear to this day that I saw Elvis in my room) and disorientation. Unlike any other incident, this was the one time that I was convinced that I would die an early death. The massive doses of antibiotics and medication to relieve both the pain and the spasms put me in a semi-conscious state, but in the middle of one night I awoke long enough to feel Fran's hand gently stroking my face and heard the words "I love you" spoken with more conviction than I had ever heard them said before. Her touch was so comforting that it made me forget about the pain my body was experiencing, and her words were as comforting as any I have ever heard. Despite the sterile, clinical setting, I felt the warmth and depth of being loved in ways that defy description.

"Love consists of this, that two solitudes protect and touch and greet each other."
—RAINER MARIA RILKE

At that moment, I knew two things: first that I would eventually be OK and second that I had to find a way to return that love to Fran. I wish that I could say that I adequately show her how much she means to me and how much I love and appreciate her every day. In some ways, I doubt that that will ever be possible, but knowing this drives me to try harder and I guess that is the point. If you really love someone, you can never do enough to show that love and repay that person for the joy they bring into your life. The key is to keep trying to do better.

"She gave me eyes, she gave me ears;
And humble cares, and delicate fears;
A heart, the fountain of sweet tears;
And love, and thought, and joy."
—WORDSWORTH
The Sparrow's Nest

Our marriage is a true partnership, and I must admit I probably got a better deal. There is little that I can or could do without Fran's love and support. She is my driver, my attendant, my lover, my partner, my editor, and my biggest critic. While she does have strong political opinions, she was not very active in campaigns and partisan politics before we were married. Now she knows just about every mover and shaker in Ohio, and they know her and her opinions.

Most importantly, we have found ways to blend our lives together in such a way as to always provide unqualified support for each other, respect each other's opinions and needs, and make room for our individual growth. If there is such a thing as a perfect marriage, it is ours.

I need to take a minute to acknowledge my first wife, Gayle. We married very young, probably without much understanding of what making a lifetime commitment to another person means. Our marriage was already in trouble when I was diagnosed with MS, but I owe Gayle a debt of gratitude for seeing me through the early years of my battle with the Beast. Most importantly, I am indebted to her for giving me two fine sons.

There are many reasons why our marriage ended. I was less than open and forthright with her and did not acknowledge or appreciate the fear and stress that my disease placed on her. I also feel that the changes that the Beast caused in our lifestyle created pressures that were too great for an already troubled relationship to handle. Despite the pain of our divorce, I left our marriage knowing a little more about myself, the importance of open and honest communication, and how my disability affected others.

As odd as it sounds, the lessons I learned from my breakup with Gayle are a big part of the foundation for the wonderful relationship I enjoy with Fran. We enjoy a deeply loving relationship that is based on honest and open communication and shared values.

"Failure is simply the opportunity to begin again, this time more intelligently." —**HENRY FORD**

CHAPTER 10

CHILDREN BRING JOY TO YOUR LIFE

ERIC AND NATHAN have touched me in much different ways but are, nonetheless, big contributors in my efforts to defeat the Beast. Like any father, I am driven by a need to do as much for them as possible and make sure that they know that they can count on my love and support. And a marvelous thing has happened as they have grown from boys into unique, individual men. They have become my friends, people to whom I would trust my life and people with whom I enjoy having long conversations about a variety of topics.

One of the greatest weapons I have to take into my battles with the Beast is an overwhelming desire to make sure that these young men are proud of me and the way I live my life. I am driven to continue to engage the Beast by a need to provide for, nourish, and protect my family.

While writing this book, I learned another lesson about children, and the Beast gets no credit for this one. My son Eric and his wife, Heather, have provided Fran and me with our first grandchild, Jaxson David Williams, and in so doing they have reminded me that it really is possible to fall in love at first sight.

"A baby is God's opinion that the world should go on."
—CARL SANDBURG

Throughout Heather's pregnancy, I felt a growing excitement that was not easy to explain. I found myself buying a baby stroller at a garage sale. I worked with friends in the prototype fabrication shop at work to develop a frame that can be affixed to my wheelchair to safely mount a child's car seat. At times it felt like Fran and I were as excited about the baby as his parents were.

I cannot find another phrase to describe the emotion of the moment just eight hours after his birth, when Eric placed Jaxson in my arms. It was love at first sight. And the joy that Jaxson brings me multiplies each time I see him. Jaxson and Grampa will be taking many walks in the park.

Jaxson's birth has made me acutely aware of the fact that there is always room in your heart to love one more child and that it is impossible to have too many children in your life. Fran and I have always made excuses to visit our nieces and nephews and, now that they are old enough, to have them stay at our home. There is something about a child's laughter, curiosity, and thirst for new information that makes life complete.

There is another lesson that I have learned from Jaxson's birth, which is to never be amazed at the wisdom and sensitivity of your grown children. Fran is not Eric's biological mother, and as Jaxson's birth approached I worried that she might be left out of some of this happy experience. To my joy and surprise, Eric and Heather had already thought about this and let us know in no uncertain terms that their child is lucky enough to have three grandmothers – each of equal status and stature. At the party celebrating Jaxson's christening, Eric actually chastised Fran for introducing herself as his "stepmother." "You are my Mom and that's it," he told her in no uncertain terms. In a very few words Eric demonstrated his maturity, told Fran that he loved her, and made his Dad very proud.

He is only 33 years old, but he is our child and our teacher. Open your heart and your mind for the lessons you will learn from the children in your lives.

CHAPTER 11

FAMILY IS THE LEAVENING THAT RAISES THE BREAD

AS ONE OF 13 CHILDREN, I find the word "family" to have many dimensions, not the least of which is that with many siblings it is easy to find some that you love not only as brother or sister but also as close friends. My "baby brother" (he hates when I refer to him this way) is a perfect example of this phenomenon.

Jim is an artist, a furniture maker whose work will take your breath away. He is always there to help with a chore I'm no longer able to do myself or to sit and chat about things of common interest. I respect him as much as any other person I know and value his insight and advice. He is a problem solver who can fashion a simple solution to what may seem to me to be an insurmountable challenge. More importantly, he has become one of my closest friends and confidants.

"My brother does not want a keeper, he wants a brother."
—MALCOLM BOYD

Jim has the uncanny ability to call at just the right time to talk about his family, politics, or what is going on in his life. He and his wife, Barb, go out of their way to include Fran and me in everything from their son Colin's school plays to picnics celebrating our nephew Aidin's birthday. Jim is a constant reminder that there is so much more to life than what I am experiencing at any one time. His most endearing trait is his ability to listen with the compassion of a priest hearing confession.

While Jim and I enjoy an especially close relationship, I

don't want to dismiss my love and appreciation for my other brothers and sisters, and, of course, my mother, Liz. In their own ways, each of them has found a way to be part of my life and thus part of the strength I bring to the battle with the Beast. Moreover, they are all constant reminders of my roots and the joys associated with growing up as part of a large family.

I have also come to realize that family is not limited to blood relatives. My "extended family" includes people I've worked with and for, neighbors, colleagues, and acquaintances. Many are as close as brothers and sisters and all are yet another source of strength. I have found that if you open your heart and mind to what other people have to offer, the size of your family can be limitless. The key is to make sure that you are honest and forthright and that you are willing to give of yourself without any expectation of receiving anything in return.

"It's easy to make a friend. You have to work at making an enemy." —**UNKNOWN**

One of the great lessons I have learned over the past few decades is the meaning of true friendship. A friend is a person who accepts you as you are, helps you when you need it, and accepts your help when they need it. It is, without question, a two-way street. Unspoken words and acts of kindness that are given without any expectation of repayment accentuate true friendships.

Clark Bruner – in fact the entire Bruner family – is the best kind of friend. He lives across the street from Fran and me and really is more like a brother than a buddy. Clark is a retired autoworker who was born and raised in rural Kentucky. His wit and humor are contagious, and it seems that he always has a story from his childhood that is relevant regardless of the topic of conversation at the moment. Most importantly, his willingness to share whatever he has with others is his hallmark. We may not have the same parents, but Clark is truly my brother.

If Mother Nature dumps a load of snow in the driveway, he is out there with his trusty snowblower clearing it away. When we travel on business, Clark, his wife Donna, or their children, Chad and Heather, take care of my fish, our cats, and Kayla, our aging dog. The Bruners do not understand how precious these gifts are to Fran and me. At the same time, Clark and Donna never hesitate to ask Fran's opinion on their gardens and landscaping or confer with me on a variety of topics. Most importantly, Clark seems to know when I am feeling a little low and finds a way to pick me up with a lively conversation about politics or an invitation to join him for a cold beer.

"A good neighbor doubles the value of your house."
—GERMAN PROVERB

This type of love is priceless. It is more important that your family and friends know that you really care about what is going on in their lives than it is for you to feel that they care about what is happening to you. The people with whom you enjoy this type of relationship are the ones you can count on for support in times of need.

Another lesson I have learned about friendship is that true friendship transcends the artificial boundaries of time and distance. Here are a couple examples of what I mean.

While serving in the Celeste Administration, Fran and I became very close friends with Pari Sabety and Mark Shanahan. Pari and Mark are two of the smartest people I know (Pari was just awarded a fellowship at the Brookings Institution). In addition to our jobs, we shared a common set of core political beliefs, an avid interest in gardening and the environment, and the joy of watching their children, Liam and Katie, grow into impressive people in their own right. When a career change caused us to move 150 miles away, our friendship continued. We only get to see them two or three times a year, but it always seems like it was just yesterday. The Sabety-Shanahans are people who I know we can count on no matter what the problem may be, to be there to help us through it regardless of distance.

Rod "Punch" Metcalf is another friend from Columbus. I really can't remember how we met, but I know it revolved around the fact that Punch, then a re-employment specialist with the Bureau of Workers Compensation, came to me because he felt the bureau was being unfair in the treatment of its clients. We quickly resolved the business matter, but a spark of friendship ignited a relationship that now spans more than 20 years. Twelve or more months may pass between my conversations with Punch, but it always feels like I had talked with him earlier that day. We have a bond of trust and a mutual respect for each other that makes time irrelevant.

Relationships like these are the antidote to friendships that require convenience for their existence. As is the case in many divorces, most of the friends that I had prior to my divorce from Gayle have drifted away, not wanting to get in the middle or to make a choice. Rather than bemoan the loss of these friendships, I would rather celebrate the friendship of people like Clark, Pari and Mark, Punch, and others.

CHAPTER 12

MY FATHER WAS RIGHT!

I AM COMFORTED by the knowledge that family and the love of family transcend all barriers. It is my privilege to know many people who have achieved fame and notoriety. But the best gift I ever received was the love of my father, Ralph E. Williams, Sr. – the greatest man I have ever met. Despite the fact that he has been dead for ten years, he is in my thoughts and drives my actions every single day. He is, in every sense of the word, my hero and was my best friend. I say that because I truly believe that it is the great accomplishments of common men and not the common accomplishments of great men that define who is and is not a hero.

After returning from World War II as a highly decorated bomber pilot, Dad entered college on the GI Bill and studied history and government. He wanted to be a teacher, but before he could finish college, he was the father of four with a fifth child (me) on the way. He had to abandon his dream of becoming a teacher for a better-paying job working for the railroad, but his thirst for knowledge, his love of history, and his intense interest in politics and government never left him.

By some stroke of good fortune, I was selected as the beneficiary of his passion, and I spent hours talking with him about history, arguing about politics, and being challenged by him to learn more and become involved. I remember with great fondness the many times when, even though we agreed, he would take the opposite side in a debate just so we could have a more lively discussion. He would also refuse to provide me the answers to questions even when I knew he had the answers. Instead, he challenged me to look them up and let him know what I had learned. He taught me the basic research skills that I continue to use every day.

As I became more politically active and especially after I was selected for a senior staff position by Governor Celeste, I found myself calling him and asking him for his thoughts and advice. To this day, the question "*How would Ralph do it?*" runs through my mind before making many major decisions. The funny thing is that the only time I remember my dad saying the words "I love you" was at the end of a phone conversation the night he died. His love lives on inside me and is a constant source of wisdom and inspiration in everything I do. His passion and strength of character embolden me to face down any challenge that life with the Beast may place before me.

Like my dad, the Beast is a good teacher. One of the most important lessons both have taught me is that everything that happens to you, good or bad, is a shared experience. It's not only I who have MS; my family and friends have also been forced to be part of my battle with the Beast. From sharing the fear of the unknown that is multiple sclerosis to making adjustments to the architecture of their homes, they too live with the Beast. At the same time, they have shared my victories and been part of the successes that I enjoy.

"Believe me, a thousand friends suffice thee not. But, in a single enemy thou hast more than enough."
—Ali Ben Abi Taleb

Experiencing all the love of my dad, Fran, my family, and dozens of friends has made me more acutely aware that nobody is ever truly alone. Like it or not, life *is* a shared experience. The decisions you make for yourself *do* have consequences for everyone you know. And, when the chips are down, there will always be someone there to offer a helping hand if you just look for it.

CHAPTER 13

NOTHING IS AS VALUABLE AS THE GIFT OF GIVING

NOTHING MAKES YOU FEEL more complete than knowing that what you are doing is helping others.

"Many people wait throughout their whole lives for the chance to be good in their own fashion."
—FRIEDRICH NIETZSCHE

As the Beast made me more and more dependent upon others to perform the routine tasks of daily life, I found it easy to discount my own contributions to society. The more others had to do for me, the more incomplete I felt as a man. However, over time I came to realize that the best way to counter this sense of loss was to make sure that I engaged in activities that helped others as much as possible.

We are made complete by that which we do for others, not what we do for ourselves.

John Vanco is the personification of this fact. John and I were classmates in a local program designed to recruit and develop the next generation of community leaders known as Leadership Lorain County. The program is nine months long and starts off with a two-day retreat for the classmates to get to know one another. As luck would have it, John and I were paired up as roommates for the retreat and have been fast friends ever since.

John underwent a mastectomy for breast cancer, a rare malady among men. In fact, the condition is so rare among men that there are no support groups for people like John. So when his search for a peer support group turned up nothing,

John was the only man to join the local breast cancer support group for women. In so doing, he educated women about how men are affected by the disease and learned a lot about how breast cancer can be devastating for women. He is now a much sought after speaker on the subject and a peer counselor for men and women diagnosed with breast cancer. The experience has made him complete not because of what he gets out of it but because of what he gives to others confronted by the disease.

John Vanco is an unassuming man who has had a profound impact on the lives of dozens of people who were overwhelmed by a frightening disease. By simply giving of himself, he has helped others come to peace in a frightening situation. By being himself he has made others courageous in the face of the unknown.

"Success is not so much in what you are, but in what you appear to be." —ANONYMOUS

Following John's example, I have become very involved in the local chapter of the National Multiple Sclerosis Society as a member of its board of directors. I also make a lot of presentations about the disease and how it changes the lives of people challenged by it as well as their families and friends. There is nothing that helps me deal with my own Beast more than educating others about the impact MS can have on the lives of patients, their families, and their friends.

More significantly, I have found that the lessons learned from my battle with the Beast are relevant to anyone who deals with adversity. Sharing my thoughts on learning from adversity makes me feel better about myself. Moreover, as I share the lessons learned from my battle with the Beast and help people understand the challenges they face, I have learned all people face different challenges everyday.

Knowing this makes me confident that I can handle any challenges my Beast may throw my way.

"No one has greater love than this, to lay down one's life for one's friends." —JOHN 15:13

No matter what challenges life may throw your way, the best way to work through them is to find a way to help someone else deal with their challenges. If you are grieving the loss of a loved one, console another grieving person. If you have experienced a business failure, learn from your mistakes and share those lessons with someone else. If you are suffering from a health problem, join a support group and share your feelings and experiences with others. These are acts of love, acts that will help make you whole again.

CHAPTER 14

BIGGER IS NOT ALWAYS BETTER

PEOPLE WASTE TOO MUCH time and energy searching for joy through expensive toys and exotic vacations. I have come to know that nothing soothes the soul as much as the sight of an eagle in flight, a field of wildflowers swaying in the breeze, a baby's smile, or the sound of the laughter of elders watching small children at play. True happiness is almost always within our reach if we just take the time to look for it.

This has not been an easy lesson to learn, and it is even harder to incorporate it into my life. I'm a guy who always looks at things from 30,000 feet. I can see the big picture – where I am and where I want to be and how to plot a course to get there. Then I become a hard driver who is terrible with detail and has little patience with people who don't see what I see. Luckily, God blessed me with some leadership and communication skills that help me compensate for my shortcomings.

Fran is an extremely talented writer who can take other people's words and thoughts – both written and oral – and make them sound better. She is also one of the best facilitators I have ever met. Lots of folks who have been in a meeting with her refer to her skills as "being able to herd cats." And yet, she can be right up against a deadline and still find time to talk to every child she sees or just walk in the garden and smell the flowers. It took me years to understand the pleasure she derives from life's small wonders. She can't drive by a herd of dairy cows without saying, "Hello, girls," or pass a hawk on a pole before saying, "Hi, handsome." (At first I thought she was talking to me, but that bubble was soon burst!) Watching how these little things give her plea-sure has been an inspiration to me.

Sports and physical activity were a major part of my life growing up. In the early 70s I rediscovered bicycling. I had a top-of-the-line touring bike and would ride 50 miles or more at a time whenever possible. Needless to say, loss of periph-eral vision and compromised balance put a serious crimp in this activity. For the longest time, the distinct sound of a line of bicyclists passing by would bring tears to my eyes.

"When one door closes another door opens; but we so often look so long and so regretfully upon the closed door that we do not see ones which open for us."
—ALEXANDER GRAHAM BELL

When I moved to Columbus to work for the governor, I met a group of guys who played wheelchair basketball and participated in road races and track and field events. I quick-ly joined and rekindled my love of sports. I never attained anything approaching world-class status, but just the act of participating filled a big void in my life. I also found that I was able to help young people master the skills of wheelchair sports and was soon demonstrating the truth of the old say-ing, "Those who can't do, coach."

At the time I started coaching, the Ohio High School Athletic Association had no program that permits kids with disabilities to participate in interscholastic sports (despite the fact that the US Olympic Committee has been doing so since 1972). That meant that these kids had no experience with competitive sports. This was unacceptable to me, and as usual I jumped in with both feet. I approached my coaching responsibilities just like any high school coach and held my athletes to the same standards of academic eligibility. I also required them to demonstrate the other behaviors most par-ents and coaches want associated with top student athletes.

They were expected to participate at every level of the sport: proper preparation and training; good sportsmanship; follow-through after an event; supporting their teammates; showing respect for their teachers, coaches, and parents; and, most importantly, demonstrating honor in their personal behavior.

Within a year after starting to coach the juniors (wheelchair sports is divided into juniors – kids ages 7 to 19 – and adults – 20 and over), a young man I had been coaching named Corey Schindler qualified to go to the National Junior Wheelchair Championships (NJWC). To qualify for these prestigious and highly competitive events, the athletes have to meet or exceed national standards for participation and performance in their chosen sport and specialty. Just getting to the NJWC was a tremendous accomplishment!

Corey surprised everyone by coming in third in the 1,500-meter race in his first year of competition. Two years later, I was coaching five young athletes who had improved their skills enough to represent Ohio at the NJWC that year. Together, they brought home 21 individual medals and the team championship trophy. I continued coaching for 7 more years and took teams to the NJWC each year.

However, my greatest accomplishment in wheelchair sports really happened almost 10 years after I had hung up my whistle for the last time.

Today, three of the kids I coached are in college – notable accomplishments on their own considering the low rates of college enrollment among kids with disabilities. This year, one of the first of "my" juniors, Nathan Pendell, graduated from the University of Illinois with honors. He was also selected to be a member of the team representing the United States in the World Team Cup games in Tokyo, Japan. More importantly, he is now in graduate school on a fellowship studying kinesiology and coaching young wheelchair athletes himself. Nate and the other young men and women and their successes represent my greatest accomplishments in wheel-chair sports.

Earlier in this book, I mentioned my last trip into the deep woods and the photograph that memorializes that event. Actually, the trip memorialized by the photo on my office wall was not my last trip to the deep woods, it was the last time I *walked* in the deep woods. In 1990, John Winters, a dear friend from Columbus who is called Henry by his close friends, invited me to join him and some of his buddies at a "wheelchair accessible" hunting cabin in the mountains of West Virginia.

Accessibility within the cabin on Jukey Ridge was marginal. The ramp was a sheet of plywood onto the porch and the "accessible restroom" was a tree into which some joker had carved the international symbol of access. I spent the first evening at camp consuming more than a few beers, enduring the usual harassment dished out to the new guy, and listening to the guys talk about how much fun I would have the next day riding the trails in an ATV equipped with hand controls.

The next morning, two guys alternately poured and pushed my butt into the ATV, strapped me in like an astronaut ready for launch, and explained how easy it is to drive the vehicle. "There are only 3 controls – the gas, the brake, and the steering wheel. Even you can handle it," they said. Before they would let me accompany them on the trails that wound through the wooded mountainside, I was told to go out in an open field and "floor it." I was roaring across the field at full throttle and having a blast when I spotted some of the guys jumping up and down and waving their arms. Next thing I saw was Henry coming at me full speed and yelling something, so I hit the brakes – just in time, it turned out. I came to a stop at the very edge of a pond that was hidden by tall grass. From that moment on, I decided that the smart thing to do was to follow someone who knew the property better than I did.

Despite my early scare, I managed to master the ATV and spent two wonderful days roaring through trails in the woods of West Virginia – what a blast and what a gift from my friend Henry. During the day, I saw deer, raccoon, and a variety of game birds. During the evening, I was introduced to real West Virginia "moonshine," which is an experience I will never forget or repeat. We sat around the camp fire and marveled at a swarm of dragonflies that looked like a battalion of hovering Blackhawk helicopters preparing for an invasion. I don't have any photos, but the memories of those three days live on. And, like the proverbial fish that got away, the stories of how fast we went and how many near disasters I encountered grow with time.

The memories of those two trips into the woods, though very different and separated by much more than mere time, remind me of how much I enjoy being outdoors and taking pictures of the outdoors. I have always enjoyed photography, in part because it is a way to compensate for my vision problems. I've replaced the subjects found in the deep woods with flowers and historic buildings. In so doing, I have rediscovered the beauty that surrounds us everyday.

> **"When you take a flower in your hand and really look at it, it is your world for the moment."**
> **—GEORGIA O'KEEFFE**

Fran is a gardener. During the holiday season, other guys spend days shopping for jewels and fancy clothes for their wives. Not me! Fran wants things like rototillers, chipper shredders, and rain barrels. Her favorite season of the year is the 2 weeks just after Christmas when the seed catalogues come in the mail by the dozens. I used to sit back and laugh at her enthusiasm for her hobby, but time has taught me that it comes from a place deep inside her that sees beauty in growing things and gains immense pleasure from sharing her knowledge of gardening with others. She does the lion's share of the work (my domain is the water garden and tending the fish), and our yard is fast becoming a showplace. We have both reached the point where spending time in the garden is more enjoyable than just about any other activity.

Our other love is the game of baseball. Fran comes from Massachusetts and grew up a Boston Red Sox fan. I, on the other hand, am a lifelong fan of the Cleveland Indians. Since both teams have a history of breaking their fans' hearts, it was easy to convince Fran to root for her new "home team." For several years, we had season tickets for the Indians but they are cost-prohibitive for us now. We still get to a few games each year but have found two substitutes that are more than adequate.

The first is to listen to the games on the radio while we sit by the pond and waterfall that are part of our garden. The other is to attend the minor league games of one of the six teams that are within 2 hours of our home. Same game, same environment at a fraction of the cost! We've discovered that minor league players approach the game with a lot more passion and enthusiasm than their major league counterparts because they are always trying to impress some scout that they are "ready for the show."

> **"The one constant through all the years has been baseball. America has rolled by like an army of steamrollers. It's been erased like a blackboard, rebuilt, and erased again. But baseball has marked the time. This field, this game, is a part of our past. It reminds us of all that once was good, and that it all can be good again."**
> **—JAMES EARL JONES as Terence Mann in the movie *Field of Dreams***

I'm sure that there are people who would describe our life as boring, but the fact of the matter is that we have found that life's true pleasures don't have to cost a ton of money, and many can be found right in your own backyard.

I know people who obsess over the fact that their boat is too small or they only get to Europe every other year. Boating, travel, and other activities are legitimate diversions from life's daily grind. But rather than waste time thinking about what they can't do or what they don't have, I encourage people to take a few minutes each day to look around and see the beauty, joy, and happiness that is right there at their fingertips. I also advise people to simplify their lives, and they will find happiness beyond all measure.

CHAPTER 15

WORK IS THE LIFEBLOOD OF HUMAN EXISTENCE

"For every man moreover, to eat and drink and enjoy the fruits of all his labor is a gift from God."
—ECCLESIASTES 3:13

MY COMEBACKS HAVE BEEN very important to me because of the strong work ethic instilled in me by my father. Dad had a good job, and he shared in the work of raising a large family, which at times was quite taxing. Food and clothes for 13 kids were not cheap, so he supplemented his income with odd jobs, installing furnaces, fixing electrical wiring in summer cottages, and doing just about any home improvement task other people would pay him to do. I would accompany him on these jobs and help out, fetching tools, running errands, and holding things in place while he worked – and gave me orders. Looking back, I now see that he took great pride in whatever job he was doing at the time. The greatest lessons he ever taught me were the value of hard work and the importance of taking responsibility for supporting yourself and your family.

I have worked since I was very young. I picked fruits and vegetables at a local commercial garden, delivered newspapers (I was once named the Pennsylvania Newspaper Publishers Association "Carrier of the Year"), and caddied at the local country club throughout high school. While in college, I started off as an orderly at a small hospital, became the assistant to the pathologist – a job that included helping perform autopsies – and eventually found a home in the developing field of nuclear medicine. I took to this new field like a duck to water and quickly developed the knowledge and skills needed to succeed in it. Within seven years, I had moved from a student at Doctor's Hospital in Erie, Pennsylvania, to the director of the department at Marymount Hospital in Cleveland. I also was elected president of the Central Chapter (seven Midwestern states) of the Technologist Section of the Society of Nuclear Medicine and was a member of the board of the national association. I am the author of several articles and have won awards for several innovative techniques and devices I invented.

Then the Beast stepped in and taught me that it is impossible for me to be at peace with myself if I don't feel that I am doing everything I can to be a productive, contributing member of society.

A serious setback landed me in the ICU for almost a month, followed up by several months in a rehab hospital from which I was discharged as a full-time wheelchair user in late 1978. While I was on sick leave, the hospital administrators, in consultation with my family lawyer, made the decision that it was no longer possible for me to function as a nuclear medicine technologist in a hospital setting. Our lawyer filed the papers with Social Security, and I was declared to be "permanently and totally disabled" and eligible for Social Security Disability Insurance, Medicare, and long-term disability benefits. I will never forget receiving the letters that said that I would never have to work another day in my life. More significantly, most of the people closest to me thought that this was a good thing!

This was a horrible message to send a person who was 29 years old. Unfortunately, it was representative of the thinking of many people in the health care field at the time. Success was measured in terms of an individual's ability to perform the activities of daily living – bathing, eating, dressing, etc. – without any consideration given to the patient's desire to return to work. I was very depressed, very lonely, and suffered from very low self-esteem. This would be true of any person who has even the smallest bit of self-respect.

Luckily, there were friends who knew my abilities, were willing to disregard my disability, and pitched in to help me find a way to regain a sense of productivity in my life.

"If you can conceive it and your heart can believe it, then you can achieve it." **—UNKNOWN**

For some people, work means heading a business that gives jobs to others, and for others it may be as simple as reading to a child. But everyone can make a contribution to society.

Some may think that this sounds strange coming from a partisan Democrat, but I believe that our society has gone too far in enabling people who are capable of working to stay at home and collect benefits – and it has not done enough to help people who really want to work to do so.

In 1986, I was invited to address the graduating class of a small school for students with disabilities. The class was only about 30 students, so I decided to forego the usual formal speech and try and engage the students in a conversation about their future. I started off by asking the kids what they were planning to do after they graduated. I was shocked to hear the majority of these bright kids say that they planned to take advantage of the Supplemental Security Income (SSI) program with its Medicaid benefit and had no plans or interest in getting jobs or furthering their education.

"Give a man a fish and he will eat for a day. Teach a man to fish and he will eat for a lifetime." **—CHINESE PROVERB**

Far worse than the choice made by these 18-year-old kids was the fact that they had made their decisions based, in part, on the advice of a professional guidance counselor.

In their defense, I have to note that unemployment among adults with disabilities who are able to work is around 65%, the highest of any demographic cohort in America. More significantly, the geniuses in Washington who keep talking about how to fix this problem seem to ignore the fact that the major reason people with disabilities are not willing to take the risk of going to work is that they do not generally have access to affordable health insurance. Pre-existing condition exclusions, the high cost for perceived high-risk beneficiaries, and the fact that many small employers don't offer employee benefits are all contributing factors. But the biggest risk is that once you go to work, you are considered to have demonstrated your ability to obtain and retain a job and are therefore generally ineligible to return to the Medicare or Medicaid safety nets.

In 1999, Congress passed the Ticket to Work and Work Incentives Improvement Act to address the barriers keeping hundreds of thousands of people with disabilities out of the workforce. However, four years later, the implementing regulations have yet to be published, and another Rose Garden signing ceremony remains nothing but an unfulfilled promise. It seems the moral imperative expressed in the legislation ran into the budget process and came out the loser. The mini-minds in Washington see only the initial costs of the program and ignore the benefit of turning tax users into taxpayers. Experience tells me that there will be some demonstration projects, and then the good intentions of a noble Congress will die on the vine of indifference.

"What does he contribute to society? A wave of his hand and a smile for every person he meets. Are these not among the most valuable gifts one person can give another?" —**ROBERT PERSKE**

Bob Perske is an internationally known author and lecturer on the subject of community integration for people with developmental disabilities. He acknowledges that there are people who have disabilities that are so complex and limiting that they are indeed unable to engage in paid employment as you and I know it. But all individuals have a right to be involved in every aspect of their community and a responsibility to be as productive as possible, to give something back to the community where they live.

As I noted earlier, it is an indictment against our society that people who do try to be involved often do so at the risk of losing the benefits they need to survive. David Jayne is a young man from Georgia who has what is commonly called Lou Gehrig's disease or amyotrophic lateral sclerosis (ALS). ALS is a rapidly progressive neurological disease that robs patients of the ability to walk, speak, or move their extremities. To deal with the day-to-day limitations of ALS, David, who is eligible for home health services, has an aide to help him with bathing, dressing, eating, etc. He, in turn, has poured every ounce of his energy into being a good father and a peer counselor for the ALS Association. David is a productive member of society even though he is not earning a paycheck.

But here is where the problem is. In the fall of 2001, some of David's college friends invited him to join them on a trip to see his alma mater play a football game. He went, and in so doing, became ineligible for Medicare coverage for his home health services. Some bureaucrat ruled that David had demonstrated that he was "able to leave the four walls of his home for a reason other than to seek medical services or attend church." His one-day journey cost him his eligibility for the services he needs to stay alive!

> **"David Jayne unselfishly gives of himself to be a good parent and to help other people diagnosed with ALS face their challenges. In turn, his government has repaid him for his courage and commitment by taking away the services he needs to survive."**
> **—CONGRESSMAN ED MARKEY (D-MA)**

Today David Jayne is on yet another journey. He is leading a nationwide effort to get this restrictive rule changed so that he and thousands of other people in similar situations can reassume their rightful places as full participants in the lives of their communities. I and many people like me are counting on him to succeed.

"One man with conviction constitutes a majority."
—Jewish Proverb

I am acutely aware that my abilities and the type of work I am able to do will continue to evolve as the Beast continues its relentless attack on my body. But I am consoled by the knowledge that every human being can give something back to the community they call "home."

"Nothing will ever be accomplished if all obstacles must first be overcome." **—E. "Pat" Nally**

Pat Nally is the retired Senior VP of Sales at Invacare. A plaque bearing the above quote was presented to me the day I started at the company. It is emblematic of the company's can-do spirit and has become a guiding philosophy during my battle with the Beast. I find that Pat's words give me confidence that, as daunting as any future challenges may be, they will take me on new paths with new challenges to overcome and new opportunities to grow.

CHAPTER 16

LIFE'S ONLY CONSTANT IS CHANGE, GET READY FOR IT!

THIS WHOLE BOOK IS ABOUT change. The fact of the matter is that change is a major component of the human condition. Everyone lives through many changes, some more difficult than others and some so intense they may be called "life altering." Change can be frightening, and surviving change requires work. It often means giving up the familiar and the comfortable for unknown and therefore frightening new realities. But change can also bring about new happiness, unanticipated efficiencies, new ideas, and other positive benefits.

The key to surviving change is to acknowledge its existence and then develop a plan for the transition from what was reality to what *is* reality. The first step in planning for a major change is to identify what has been altered. Don't waste a lot of time waiting for things to return to the familiar.

"When you face a great challenge, look at it, size it up and make a decision. Don't postpone your life just because you can't make up your mind."
—GENERAL OMAR BRADLEY

For example, after years of fighting it, I finally gave in to the advice of my medical team (and some very knowledgeable friends) five years ago and switched from using a manual wheelchair to a power chair. The thinking was that power would help me conserve my increasingly limited energy for more important things than moving from one place to another. Some people may think of this as insignificant, but it was a huge change that required some major adjustments in my life.

A properly fit manual wheelchair really becomes part of your body, and after a while maneuvering it through life requires little thought. A power chair is a complex machine, and it requires months, even years, to become a proficient and confident driver. The change is very similar to the difference between walking and driving a car.

Once the change is identified, you have to begin thinking of how it will impact every other aspect of your life. With my manual chair, I was able to transfer from the chair to the car seat, and Fran could easily load the chair into the trunk. The switch to power required the purchase of a lift-equipped van, a vehicle that costs as much as a luxury car and drives like a truck. Our home was fairly accessible, but we did have to do some additional modifications to doorways and the bathroom to accommodate a wider, longer power chair that is more difficult to turn. The good news is that power-chair technology is changing rapidly, reducing chair size and dramatically improving maneuverability.

We also had to make some changes in our social life. The manual chair was easy for friends to lift with me in it so no one's house was off limits. The power chair is a different story. Before going anywhere, we have to check on accessibility and we now carry around a set of portable ramps that can transform a couple of porch steps into an accessible entrance. As my arm strength continues to decrease, I have more difficulty transferring out of the chair and have had to learn how to reposition myself to avoid pressure sores. Fran has also had to master different ways to help me transfer and to pull me into proper position when fatigue causes my muscles to fail.

The reason I fought the transition to powered mobility was, in large measure, that it was a very visible admission that the Beast was gaining on me. The psychological impact of this change has been far more difficult to deal with than anything else.

Mark Sullivan is a colleague at Invacare who lives in our neighborhood. When I was using a lightweight manual chair, I frequently caught a ride to work with him. Let me rephrase that: I frequently *tried* to catch a ride to work with him. "Sully" has a small memory problem, and, even though I would call him as he was leaving his house and remind him to pick me up, there was more than one occasion when I found myself sitting on the driveway watching him drive by, oblivious to the fact that I was waiting for him. I had better luck getting rides home because I would literally take his car keys from him.

Aside from the adventure associated with this memory problem, there was a very real social aspect of riding with Sully that is now impossible. During the 20-minute commutes, we talked about our kids, sports, our shared interest in photography, and a variety of topics. It was time alone with a friend that I took for granted until the Beast made it impossible to continue. We are still friends and Sully still visits, but like so many other personal interactions, the spontaneity of our relationship is gone.

In my opinion, the very worst aspect of my battles with the Beast is that nearly every aspect of my life now has to be planned out ahead of time. In second place is the fact that everything takes so much more time and energy.

The most exhausting thing I have to do everyday is get up, shower, shave, brush my teeth, and get dressed. What most guys do in 15 minutes takes me an hour or two of hard work, more if my bowels need coaxing or my urostomy appliance must be changed. Most days I require help getting dressed in the morning (the good news is that my selection of colors is less likely to clash) and undressed at night. I try very hard not to have to change clothes during the day.

There have been numerous other aspects that have had to be addressed because of the changes imposed on me by the Beast. But the point is that it is easier to accept changes if you think through all the possible ways change will affect your life and the lives of the people around you and find ways to address them.

"Morale is a state of mind. It is steadfastness and courage and hope." —GENERAL GEORGE C. MARSHALL

I can see more changes coming as the Beast continues its relentless intrusion into my life. By acknowledging this fact, Fran and I are able to plan for the transitions that may be necessary. The progressive loss of fine motor control in my hands will undoubtedly lead to a time when my ability to use a computer keyboard will be very limited. In anticipation of this, I have begun using voice recognition software that transfers speech into text. Much of this book has been dictated to the computer rather than typed in one letter at a time. When a computer keyboard is no longer an option, I'll be ready and able to continue to use my computer.

"Procrastination is the art of keeping up with yesterday." —DON MARQUIS

A planned transition makes things easier to accept, and the outcomes are more likely to be positive than negative. Naturally, it is easier to plan for a change when you know it is coming.

A few years back, Fran and I added a water garden to our landscaping, and it has been a big part of my springs, summers, and autumns ever since. The way ours is situated, I am able to do much of the work it takes to maintain the 8' by 12' by 4' deep body of water we call "Lake Dave." I get a lot of pleasure out of preparing the marginal plants for positioning each spring, repotting the water lilies, and managing the chemical balance of this little ecosystem. But the part I enjoy most of all is tending to the 30+ fish that populate the pond.

I must point out that these are not your ordinary "gold-fish." Our pond is stocked with several varieties of ornamental koi, sarasas, calico fantails, and multi-colored shubunkens, each fish more beautiful than the other. Twice a day, I roll up to the water's edge and the magic begins. The older fish know me on sight and race over to be fed, followed soon thereafter by the younger fish. The sight of them approaching washes away the nagging worries of my worst days.

Like most things I take up, I immersed myself in this hobby with great intensity. When fall came, I found myself dreading the onset of the North Coast winters when the fish would go deep and the pond would freeze over. Then I realized that this is a change that was going to happen each year and, with a little research, I could develop a plan to handle it. Now when the fall comes, I switch my attention to the 100-gallon aquarium in my office that serves as an incubator for future residents of Lake Dave. It is not the same, but it sure makes a difference. Like the pond, tending the aquarium and watching the fish get ready to join their relatives when spring comes around has its own calming effect on me.

"Remember, it wasn't raining when Noah built the ark." —**HOWARD RUFF**

The next time you see a big change coming in your life, see if you can develop a plan to bring your own water garden inside for the winter.

CHAPTER 17

LEARN FROM YOUR MISTAKES AND FAILURES

"Only those who dare to fail greatly can ever achieve greatly."   —ROBERT F. KENNEDY

WE ALL MAKE mistakes. Wars have been fought over mistakes and misunderstandings between nations. Congress has passed laws before realizing that there was no money to pay for them. Kids actually do leave their homework on the kitchen table. The key for everyone is to learn from their mistakes.

The first step in learning from our mistakes is to acknowledge that we have made them and take responsibility for our actions.

"... life breaks us all but afterward many become strong at the broken places."   —ERNEST HEMINGWAY
A Farewell to Arms

Mistakes often stem from weaknesses – real or perceived. Like exercising to increase the muscle mass around an injured bone, these are some of the best places to build strengths. Let me give you an example.

Two of my problems are a loss of peripheral vision and diminished fine motor control in my hands. Combined, they create a significant weakness in my ability to get around (you only need to look at the woodwork in our home to see the truth in that statement). Operating a power wheelchair requires good hand-eye coordination and a lot of practice. Take a turn too quickly, scratch the baseboard. Go too slowly and you nick the doorjamb. I have made a lot of mistakes as I have tried to master the fine art of driving a power wheelchair, but I have also made a conscious effort to try not to make the same mistake twice. In so doing, I have learned to think ahead and plan my movements so that I can execute them smoothly. Why? Because it looks bad for an executive of the company manufacturing the wheelchair to be seen careening off the walls like he's had one too many shots of scotch!

"Success is never final. Failure is never fatal. It's the courage to try that counts!" —COACH JOHN WOODEN

Seriously, as I work to master the art of planning ahead for the movements of my chair, I have begun to apply the same principles to other aspects of my life. Now when I leave the house I think of where I'm going to be and what I may have to do before I get back. Then I make sure I have all the tools, information, and supplies I may need before I get back home. Not only does this make me look like I'm organized, but it also allows me to be a little more independent and flexible, which is a major improvement over my previously disorganized persona.

"Failure is the condiment that gives success its flavor." —TRUMAN CAPOTE

No matter how hard we work, regardless of how noble our intention, part of the human condition is to fall short of our goals or to fail altogether. But only fools fail to pursue something new because they are afraid that they might fail achieving it. None of us knows how far we can go or how much we can achieve until we try.

"The question should be, is it worth trying to do? Not, can it be done?" —ALLARD LOWENSTEIN

There is not a day that goes by when one of the Beast's calling cards (a.k.a. symptoms) does not cause me to wonder whether or not I will be able to do something. If there are three inches of snow on the ground, will I be able to get to the curb to get the newspaper? If there are important meetings six hours apart, will I have the stamina to make it to both of them? If the laundry needs folding and Fran has had a long day, can I do it without too much pain setting in?

Applying "Lowenstein's principle" helps me make those decisions and make adjustments when necessary. The paper can wait; that's why God inspired Ted Turner to invent CNN. I can do both meetings if I just find a way to lie down for a couple of hours in between. And the laundry, well, I hate folding laundry anyway, so I'll take a pass on that one. I know Fran won't mind, and lots of people live out of the laundry basket instead of the closet.

> **"Concern yourself not with what you tried and failed in, but with what it is possible for you to do."**
> **—POPE JOHN XXIII**

One of the big reasons I fail, or at a minimum fail to provide my best effort, is that one of the hardest things for me to do is to say "no" when someone asks me to do a favor, challenges me with a new opportunity, or tempts me with an opportunity to learn something new. As I've told you earlier, I have limited energy reserves, and fatigue only makes things worse.

> **"All the mistakes I ever made were when I wanted to say no and instead said yes."**   **—MOSS HART**

You may not have MS or any other disability, but all of us must accept the fact that there are only 24 hours in a day, even though for some of us it seems like there are fewer. Overextending yourself can only lead to frustration and, eventually, to failure. I wish I could tell you that I've mastered this lesson. I've learned it, but I must be honest and tell you that I'm not very good at it. I have to develop a mindset that it is better to do fewer things very well than it is to do a lot of things adequately.

"No one learns to make good decisions without being free to make bad ones." —UNKNOWN

Fear of failure used to be one of my most limiting problems. I believed that if I tried something and failed it would be attributed to my disability and evoke pity. It was easier not to try than to risk failure. I learned that I was wrong the first time I ran for public office. I lost the election, but instead of pity I found people (even some who voted against me) commenting on my courage and encouraging me to run again.

"Take chances. Make mistakes. That's how you grow. Pain nourishes your courage. You have to fail in order to practice being brave." —MARY TYLER MOORE

Be realistic when setting goals or establishing expectations. Once you reach a goal or meet expectations, raise the bar and start over. Always remember the instructions on how to eat an elephant – one bite at a time.

CHAPTER 18

THE PRINCIPLES OF LEADERSHIP

JUST WHEN I THOUGHT that this book was complete, I agreed to take part in an "appreciative inquiry" session with the new class of our local community leadership development program – Leadership Lorain County (LLC). I did it as a member of the LLC class of 1994 and as a representative of Invacare, one of the largest employers in the county. I am certain that I got much more out of the experience than the class did. I came away wondering if I was worthy of being considered a "community leader" and, if I was, what made me so, and how it was that I became a "leader."

I never considered myself to be a leader while growing up. I equated leadership with status – money, athletic ability, and even relationships to other leaders. In college, I came to equate leadership with authority and knowledge and often confused it with the command structure I was exposed to as an ROTC cadet. I disagree with the often repeated assertion that "leaders are born, not made" just as much as I question the concept of training leaders. Rather, it is my belief that, faced with the opportunity to become a leader, some people will rise to the occasion and others won't.

"When in charge, ponder. When in trouble, delegate. When in doubt, mumble." —JAMES BOREN

Ironically, it was after the Beast had begun its relentless attack on my body that I began to recognize what leadership meant and to develop my own principles of leadership. Nuclear medicine was establishing itself as an important clinical discipline around the same time I was diagnosed. This new recognition led to the development of professional standards and a professional organization. What is unique about nuclear medicine is that the entity representing the technologists developed within the group representing the physicians – the Society of Nuclear Medicine.

The founders of the local chapter of the Technologist Section of the Society of Nuclear Medicine were experiencing burnout or were moving on to new jobs in distant locations. A leadership vacuum occurred, and I was sucked in to fill the void. Failure was not an option, so I had to quickly develop my own leadership style.

Something must have worked because within two years I was president of the regional organization (covering the Great Lakes states) and a member of the national board of the society. At that point I realized that I had earned the respect of my peers and developed the skills to be recognized as a leader. Since then, I have sought out leadership opportunities in every organization I have become associated with: Rotary, the MS Society, various industry trade associations, and my parish, to name a few.

But until the Leadership Lorain County interview, I would never have described myself as a leader. Rather, I would have told you that I was "very involved in" a number of organizations in both my work and private life.

As I began reflecting on leadership, I came to realize that there is a significant difference between leadership and command. Command is necessary in a structured organization such as the military, where a commander must get his subordinates to do things that pose personal risks or philosophical conflict. It requires the existence of a set of conventions that define who can issue a command (rank, written rules, etc.) and how that command is to be followed. Orders must be given, and subordinates must follow those orders to the letter.

Leadership is a much different animal. A leader is a person who can get a group of individuals to come together voluntarily and take collective ownership and responsibility for a task or series of tasks leading toward a shared goal. A leader has no subordinates but rather has been selected, often by default, to guide equals on a journey towards their goal.

"I am more afraid of an army of 100 sheep led by a lion than an army of 100 lions led by a sheep."
—C.M. DE TALLEYRAND

People follow a commander out of fear. A leader motivates followers to share a vision, agree to goals, and develop plans for achieving those goals. A leader can't dictate either policy or practice. Instead, a leader facilitates the process of building group consensus and individual ownership of both the process and the objective.

Although I suspect that the faculties of West Point and Annapolis might disagree with them, I have my own set of effective leadership principles. Don't get me wrong; I believe that many military commanders are also leaders, just as many volunteer leaders confuse their roles with those of a military commander. True leadership happens whether you are a commander or a leader.

Here are my personal principles of leadership. These have worked well for me, but you may need to add to or modify them as you find yourselves in positions of leadership. They reflect the fact that I prefer to work in team settings where a group is working toward a common goal or objective. Further modification may be necessary for different situations. I'll tell you up front that the hardest thing about being a leader is acknowledging that there are times when you must set your leadership style aside, make a tough decision, and then help the group to accept that decision as its own.

- Leaders have more respect for the people who follow them than they would expect them to have for their leader.

- Leaders never ask a follower to do anything that the leader is unwilling to do himself or herself.

- Leaders do not allow their followers to fail. When there is a mistake, it must be seen as a learning opportunity and not a sign of failure.

- Leaders never say "I." Rather, leaders always refer to themselves and their followers as "we."

- A leader never takes personal credit for what the collective group has accomplished.

- At the same time, a leader shoulders all the responsibility for success and is willing to accept any and all the criticism of the group and/or any individual member of the group.

- A leader, with the active input of the group, is responsible for creating a vision and then making certain that this vision is understood and accepted by every member of the group as their own.

- A leader is flexible and willing to listen to the ideas and criticisms of those he or she is leading and either incorporates this input into the group plan or explains why it may or may not be appropriate.

- A leader is patient and willing to invest the time it takes to build cohesion and a common sense of purpose among the group he or she is leading.

- Most importantly, a leader is a teacher who is never too busy to take the time to work with the group or any of its members to build understanding or develop the skills needed for the group's vision to become reality.

I truly believe that everyone is capable of providing leadership in one way or another and disagree with those who explain away failure by saying that there are "too many chiefs and not enough Indians." Probably the most important trait of successful leaders is that they have enough control over their egos to share any leadership roles with others. When they do, everybody wins.

"There is no substitute for a clear vision and a decisive direction." —**DICK MORRIS**
Political Strategist

So I thank the Leadership Lorain County class of 2004 for stimulating the reflection that reminded me that I am a leader. Knowing this makes me aware of my responsibility to use my leadership skills in service to my community.

CHAPTER 19

STAY TRUE TO YOURSELF

THE BEAST HAS NOT CHANGED the fact that I am an educated, opinionated, and passionate person who likes to be involved in a variety of activities and organizations and assume a leadership role when possible. I suppose many people would label me a control freak and counsel me that it is the Beast who is now in control of my life. Bunk! Not even the Beast can take away the principles and beliefs that I have built my life around.

I am passionate about politics and lean to the left when it comes to public policy, although as I grow older I do find myself becoming more conservative about government spending. It's not that the government is spending too much, it is simply that it spends too much on certain things and not enough on the needs of disadvantaged people. I'm also concerned about the mounting debt that will be passed on to my grandson and future generations. But I digress.

"Do not worry about the world coming to an end today. It is already tomorrow in Australia."
—CHARLES M. SCHULZ

Just as each of us must be able to conduct an inventory of our skills, abilities, and interests to make a comeback, we must also inventory our core beliefs and operational principles on a regular basis because these are the things against which we must measure our every action. Don't get me wrong; some values can be flexible, and many appear to change with time and experience. Still, they are the filters that we use to make tough decisions. To function effectively, they must be clear, defensible, and understandable. It is not easy to stay true to one's core beliefs, especially when you are in the minority and they are challenged regularly.

"We must adjust to changing times and still hold to unchanging principles." —**PRESIDENT JIMMY CARTER**

I have several friends who are wealthy Republicans who truly believe that government has two functions – the national defense and highway maintenance. (That may be an oversimplification, but you get my point.) One of their core values is an unbridled belief that the free-market system can solve all our nation's problems if the government would just get out of the way. Poverty would disappear, schools would improve, and the air and water would magically become clear, clean, and unpolluted.

On the other hand, I, a proud Democrat, think that the government is not doing enough to insure that every American has access to effective, affordable health care, to improve our system of public schools so that kids graduating from high school have the necessary skills to succeed in a job with a future, and to clean up our environment. I am convinced that if these matters are left to be resolved by free-market forces, the bottom line of the balance sheet will become the ultimate arbiter.

To tell you the truth, I'm not sure who is right, and I'm glad that there are at least two different opinions because the answer probably lies somewhere in the middle. But if the people in either camp abandon their principles and ignore their core beliefs, nothing will ever get done.

"If you are not a liberal when you are 20, you don't have a heart. If you are not a conservative by the time you reach 40, you don't have a brain."
—**SIR WINSTON CHURCHILL**

Churchill may have been right, but I am well over 40, believe I still have a brain, and do not see where dismantling the government just because some think it is "too big" helps build a better society or a better economy.

One of the best ways to grow as a person is to engage in conversations with people who hold differing beliefs. As a college student, I took a course in the philosophy of communism. It just so happens that I was in college during the height of the Vietnam War and had several friends fighting there. I was also in ROTC (Reserve Officers Training Corps) in the United States Army. I was confronted by the colonel who ran the ROTC program on campus and told that "taking the course was unpatriotic given that American boys were dying at the hands of communists as we speak." I responded that more people needed to understand communism if the nation was ever to defeat it. The remainder of the conversation was brief and can't be repeated in mixed company, but I believe that I was right then, and I am glad to this day that I stuck out that course. My only regret is that I received a "C" for my efforts.

"The wishbone will never replace the backbone."
—WILL HENRY

I love politics. I love public service. I am an unabashed, flag-waving patriot and an active, involved, and passionate Democrat.

I work, rather successfully, in an arena dominated (for the time being) by Republicans. I am proud of the fact that many prominent members of the GOP are friends with whom I share mutual respect: former Senator Bob Dole, Congressman Dave Hobson (R-OH), and many others. That respect is based on the fact that we all acknowledge that we each have and hold strong core beliefs and are willing to stand by and defend them even as we work through compromises that, in the end, are good for everyone.

The role-playing debates I had with my father prepared me well for the discussions I must have with members of the loyal opposition. They also remind me that one of the best aspects of active involvement in our participatory democracy is knowing that just because you disagree with someone does not mean they are always wrong. Working through political disagreements has resulted in some pretty fantastic decisions by government at every level. It does not happen all the time (less often when one party controls everything), but when it does it is a beautiful thing to see.

The same is true for life in general. If you write off everyone you disagree with, you will never learn to compromise. The ability to compromise is an essential skill no matter what endeavor you are involved in.

CHAPTER 20

DREAM BIG DREAMS

"The slow fuse of the possible is lit by the burning embers of the imagination." —EMILY DICKINSON

I BELIEVE THAT ONE of nicest things anyone can say about you is that you are a dreamer. Dreamers and visionaries are the engines that drive all progress. The Founding Fathers dreamed that they could create one country out of 13 independent, former British colonies. Today, the United States is the greatest country in the world. Henry Ford dreamed that he could make and mass market automobiles and in so doing changed the world forever.

President John F. Kennedy dreamed that man would one day walk on the moon, and his dream soon became a national obsession. Who can forget Neil Armstrong's words as he made the dream of an entire nation come true: "One small step for man, one giant leap for mankind." Dreams are very powerful things.

My successes prior to the time when the Beast entered my life were based on the belief that there was nothing I could not do if I just put my mind to it. My ambitions were fueled by dreams of new ways to use the knowledge, skills, and talents that God had given me. After the Beast had his way with me in 1978, I stopped dreaming about the future. I was so focused on what I could no longer do that I would not allow myself to dream about what I might be able to do. It was a pretty depressing time.

I had just about given up on life when a psychologist friend told me to let go of the negative and allow myself to dream again. She told me that, if I wanted to regain my self-esteem, I had to allow myself to dream and use those dreams to plot a new course for my life. It turned out to be some of the best advice I ever received.

**"Hold fast to dreams
For if dreams die
Life is a broken-winged bird
That cannot fly."**
            —LANGSTON HUGHES
            Poet & Philosopher

As you would expect, my first dreams were about what I knew best and how I could apply my skills and abilities in a productive way. I was trained and certified in the fields of radiology, nuclear medicine, and medical radiation health physics. All my work experience was in a clinical setting, but I dreamed that people would pay to know what I had learned in this relatively new clinical discipline. That dream turned into a part-time job with a consulting firm where one of my tasks was to write and produce a newsletter and conduct educational programs for aspiring technologists and physicians.

That effort put a little wind under my wings, and I began to dream about doing something in the field of politics, a subject that I had loved ever since my early discussions with my father. I became a precinct committeeman, then a member of the county executive committee, and eventually got involved in planning and executing campaign strategies for a variety of local candidates. That led to a role in the gubernatorial campaign of Dick Celeste and, after a loss the first time around, a spot on his senior staff when he was elected in a landslide in 1982.

"Dreams are like the stars. Try as he may, man may never reach them but, like the ancient mariner he is guided by them."   **—MONTAIGNE**

Dreams can be a pathway to new opportunities and success. There are always a lot of people around who are willing to tell you what you should do, but dreams help you identify what you might do. When I became disabled, people seemed to come out of the woodwork to tell me what I could no longer do, but my dreams spurred me on to try new things and to find ways to do exactly what the naysayers said I could not accomplish.

Well-meaning professionals decided in 1978 that I could no longer work, but I constantly dreamed of working again, and I have worked ever since. In the 25 years since then, I have accomplished many things and have met and worked with people of all kinds. I have come to know and understand things that are not understandable to most people, and I've learned how to make the confusing clear. I would not trade a minute of these years for anything and am very aware that none of this would have happened if I had not allowed myself to shake the bonds of doubt and self-pity and start to dream again.

There is another important aspect of dreams that I learned from Fran, which has helped me stave off some of the challenges of the Beast. I always thought that spending a lot of time daydreaming or analyzing the dreams that come during the night was not productive. Quite the opposite is true. Further, there are dreams that happen despite yourself while you are awake. You just have to be attuned to them.

Fran is a master of this practice. She has a number of sayings that she calls "family mottoes." Some of them stem from the family of her mother and father; others come from the family that is us. At any rate, she has a lot of them and she never hesitates to pull one out when it seems appropriate. One of her most frequently uttered mottoes is "Dreams are cheap." She means that it doesn't cost a cent to dream – much less to dream big.

Among the many profound thinkers that influence her life (I have learned not to question the roots or value of her wisdom) is Kermit the Frog, a Muppet created by the late Jim

Henson. In one of the Muppet movies, Kermit leads the gang in a song for dreamers entitled "The Rainbow Connection." Most folks probably think of it as a children's song with little relevance in the adult world. Wrong! "The Rainbow Connection" tells about the importance of dreams as we search for wisdom and understanding, and it is relevant to people of all ages.

> **"Why are there so many songs about rainbows and what's on the other side? Rainbows are visions, but only illusions, and rainbows have nothing to hide. So we've been told, and some choose to believe it. I know they're wrong, wait and see. Someday we'll find it, the rainbow connection, the lovers, the dreamers, and me."**
>
> **—KERMIT THE FROG**
> **in Jim Henson's *The Muppet Movie***

The more we would hear the song, the more important it became to us. In fact, "The Rainbow Connection" became emblematic of our relationship with each other to the point that, when we were married, we asked that it be played as our recessional hymn. Unfortunately, it was deemed not to qualify as "sacred music" and therefore could not be part of our wedding service. We settled for "Variations on the Canon in D" by Pachelbel, and each wore a small Kermit pin on our wedding clothes. The decoration on the top of our wedding cake (which Fran made) featured not one but two Kermit figures. One was wearing a red cummerbund and a red bow tie (guess who that one symbolized?). The other wore red shoes – yep, my bride had red snakeskin high heels on, and she clicked them together at the end of the ceremony and whispered to me, "We're not in Kansas anymore, Toto." And to further make her point, she had them sitting in rocking chairs on a platform of sand (beach) with sea gulls swirling overhead, because that's how we envisioned our retirement. Of course, it looks more like we'll be sitting next to Lake Dave with the swallows and nighthawks circling overhead, but, hey, you get the point.

"It isn't a calamity to die with dreams unfulfilled, but it is a calamity not to dream." —MAX CLELAND

My dreams are now centered around maintaining my status as an elder statesman in the home medical equipment industry. I plan to do this by writing and speaking as the practical conscience of the industry. Other dreams center around Jaxson, becoming a better photographer, and, of course, continuing to serve on city council. I also dream about how I can continue to assist Mal and Invacare in their position as the recognized leaders of the industry when it comes to political and legislative strategy. I have a lot to do, and all of it is important to me. All of it is also the subject of frequent dreams.

Make time in your life to dream. Don't limit your dreams to the possible or the familiar, but think outside those boxes and imagine grand things. If your dreams result in ideas and concepts that are sound, you will find a way to make them become reality. I'll never again be convinced that taking the time to sit by a babbling brook and allowing the mind to wander is wasted time.

"The future belongs to those who believe in the beauty of dreams." —ELEANOR ROOSEVELT

CHAPTER 21

LOW EXPECTATIONS ARE A SELF-FULFILLING PROPHECY

"Anyone who thinks they are too small to make a difference has never tried to fall asleep with a mosquito in the room."
—Former Governor CHRISTIE TODD WHITMAN

THE LESS YOU EXPECT of yourself, the less you will accomplish. If you don't think you can do it, you probably can't. If you don't set goals for yourself, you will not grow personally or professionally.

Low expectation is the identical twin to low self-esteem, which is one of the most detectable emotions. Other people can sense low self-esteem as readily as they can sense when the sun is bright. Your low self-esteem is almost immediately translated into a lack of confidence in your skills and abilities and is a huge barrier to building relationships.

"The willingness to accept responsibility for one's own life is the source from which self-respect springs."
—JOAN DIDION

I stopped believing in myself around the same time in 1978 that I was told that I could no longer work because of the limits the Beast had brought into my life. I was still the same person, knew the same things, and had the same skills, but I could no longer walk or position patients. Uncharacteristically, I accepted the idea that I would be unable to use my assets in a productive way. I began to think of myself as both a failure and a drain on my family in particular and on society in general. I could see my depression and self-loathing in the eyes of others and my sons. I soon came to realize that I had to find a way to believe in myself again or die of depression.

"It's courage and character that make the difference between players and great players; between great surgeons and the ones who bury their mistakes."
—Coach Pete Carril

Somehow I realized that I had to find the courage to identify and define what the real limits were on my life, and to differentiate between what I was told I could not do and what I was truly unable to do. Next I realized that once limits were defined, they had to be challenged because challenging them on a regular basis enabled me to constantly find ways to eliminate the perceived limit or redefine it.

I had a good understanding of both the clinical applications and the regulatory requirements associated with nuclear medicine and diagnostic radiology (X-ray). Two of my mentors, Paul Early and Bill Miller, had a consulting firm that focused on regulatory compliance for hospitals and clinics. As luck would have it, they had their offices within a block of my home. After a few conversations, we identified some services that I could perform – survey instrument calibration and writing articles for the client newsletter – and I was soon making my way back into the workforce. Within months, I was developing training seminars and giving presentations. I earned the opportunity to contribute to two textbooks that Paul was writing.

Challenging your limits – some call it pushing the envelope – is the key to finding ways to deal with a limit or get around it.

At the time, I wished that I had been given the opportunity to return to a clinical setting because I missed the opportunity to work with patients, but in hindsight I can now see that the change forced me to identify and strengthen other skills and talents that have enabled me to make the transition to a whole new area of work. Paul and Bill gave me the opportunity to polish my writing skills and forced me to become a good teacher and public speaker. These skills served me well when I made the career change from nuclear medicine to political appointee and again from advisor to the governor to being a lobbyist for Invacare.

Paul and Bill gave me the opportunity to transition from a state of low self-esteem to believing in myself and being proud of my accomplishments. More importantly, they gave me a foundation upon which I could rebuild my life. What a gift!

"Real difficulties can be overcome. It is only the imaginary ones that are unconquerable."
—THEODORE VAIL

One of the lessons I have learned from the Beast is that personal pride and happiness are based in the ongoing effort to improve yourself. It is hard to be happy if you are not moving forward, if you are not learning new things. Further, like low self-esteem, personal pride and self-confidence are clear to everyone you meet and serve as the keys to new opportunities.

As I deal with the numerous challenges the Beast has laid in my path, I am constantly reminded that learning *is* a life-long experience. I have always been a voracious reader, consuming biographies and books on politics and history like a bat eats mosquitoes. (A common bat will eat its own weight in mosquitoes each night – yum!) I also read five newspapers a day (three local papers and the *New York Times* and *Washington Post* on-line editions), paying particular attention to the stories on politics as well as the editorial pages. Add to all this *The Progressive, Mother Jones, The Nation, The New Republic, Roll Call, The Hill,* and *The New Yorker* and I get pretty broad exposure to almost every angle of political philosophy. In the process of all this reading, I have been exposed to the wit, philosophy, and wisdom of great people and great writers.

"I have seen hypocrisy that was so artful that it was good judgment to be deceived by it." —H.W. SHAW

In an effort to learn something from everything I read, I started collecting quotes (many of which appear in this book) on index cards filed in a box on my desk labeled "the Box of Wisdom." Watching for quotes to add to *the Box* is one way I remind myself to keep looking for new experiences and new learning opportunities.

I firmly believe that the minute you decide that you have nothing more to learn is the exact minute you begin to die. Since I'm not interested in dying just yet, I guess I'll just keep looking for new things to learn, and I suggest that each of you do the same.

There are no guarantees that you will succeed at everything you try, but the best insurance you can get for success is to set high goals for yourself. Goals of all kinds should be SMART – that is, Specific, Measurable, Achievable, Relevant, and Timely. Vague goals are rarely achieved, so take the time to think things through and clearly define a goal before you set it for yourself. Saying that your goal is to be a better person is too vague; saying that you are going to be a better person by performing two acts of charity a week is a SMART goal. It is specific and measurable – two acts of charity each week. It is achievable because even the busiest person can take five minutes a day to help another person or support a worthy cause. Its relevance lies in the fact that we all want to do unto others as we would have others treat us in the same situation. Finally, it is timely because it is always time to help a person in need.

Examples of other SMART personal goals might include completing an educational program, reading a book a week, or even reducing the burden of your significant other by sharing in the household chores. That last example is one I set for myself each time I revise my life plan, but it seems that I always come up short on the "measurable" test. But I will keep it as a goal because it makes me think about ways to help out around the house.

> **"Nobody makes a greater mistake than he who did nothing because he could only do a little."**
> **—Sir Edmund Burke**

Goals should not be seen as destinations but as mile markers on the endless journey of life. Goals are useless unless they are replaced with new, loftier goals once they are achieved. I have a friend whose major goal in life was to run a marathon in under three hours. Once he achieved that goal, he stopped running and became rather sedentary. He is now 40 pounds overweight, and his new goal is to lose 50 pounds in 12 months. I personally think he would be much happier if, after he had run the marathon, he had set a new personal goal of running a shorter race at a faster pace.

In 1980, I set a personal goal of returning to work full time despite the advice of many clinicians. It took three years and getting a friend elected governor to achieve that goal, but I did it. Achieving that goal has given me the courage to set new ambitious goals that run counter to the Beast's endless attacks on my body. The book that you are holding in your hand is a demonstration of what you can accomplish if you set a goal and strive to achieve it.

Having goals and making progress toward them is a tremendous source of self-confidence and self-esteem. The act of conducting regular self-assessments and setting new goals is the foundation for personal growth. We can all build on that foundation by accepting and acting on the fact that learning is a lifelong experience.

> **"We shall shoot for the stars. The worst that can happen is that we may fall a little short of the mark. But, in the process we will find out just how much we can achieve."** —GOVERNOR RICHARD F. CELESTE
> *Inaugural Address, January 1983*

As you go about setting your own goals and your personal plan for success, you must keep in mind that there are some things that are not appropriate. Building goals in such a way that achieving them comes at the expense of another person is not goal setting; it is waging war against another human being. Take care to ensure that your successes do not depend upon the failure of others. That is not to say that competition is bad. Rather, competing for the same objective must be done fairly and with respect for your competitors. When setting and reviewing goals, these words first spoken by one of America's greatest presidents (a liberal Republican) might be helpful.

THE "CANNOTS"

You cannot bring about prosperity by discouraging thrift.

You cannot help small men by tearing down big men.

You cannot strengthen the weak by weakening the strong.

You cannot lift the wage earner by pulling down the wage payer.

You cannot keep out of trouble by spending more than your income.

You cannot further the brotherhood of man by inciting class hatred.

You cannot establish security on borrowed money.

You cannot build character and courage by taking away man's initiative and independence.

You cannot help men permanently by doing for them what they could and should do for themselves.

—President Abraham Lincoln

CHAPTER 22

MAKE PEACE WITH GOD

"What you choose to believe in will drive your emotions, behavior, and thus, the results of your life."
—ART BERG
CEO, Invictus Corp.

I BELIEVE THAT THE WORLD is too complex for any reasonable person not to believe that there is a higher power. Given that, it is easy for me to say that I believe in God and practice that belief as a Christian, in fact, as a Roman Catholic. If you asked me to simplify the complex rules of Catholicism into three precepts, they would be that Jesus Christ was sent by God to live among us and teach mankind the way to eternal salvation; that the "way" to salvation is through Jesus Christ and living your life in service to God through service to mankind; and that we honor God by honoring his son Jesus Christ.

This is not to say that my faith is the only faith or that my beliefs are the only path to salvation – another term for eternal peace. I have great respect for people who perceive or worship God under different sets of rules or practices. I have friends who are Jews, Buddhists, Muslims, and a spectrum of other religions. What we all share is a fundamental belief that there is a God and that God's love is both infinite and indescribable. That recognition of God's love leads to the inevitable and inescapable understanding that we have a responsibility to return that love – to God and to others – in every aspect of our lives. We believe that in so doing, we will be rewarded by eternal peace.

The Catholic Church, like most other religious institutions, provides a set of basic beliefs and practices – I think of them as minimum standards – and suggests that you live your life in concert with this program. But as in most aspects of life, you can do the minimum and get by, or you can exceed the minimum and reap great rewards. As with most things in my life, my search is for ways to exceed the minimums, to achieve excellence, in my relationship with God. This is a lofty goal that I may never achieve, but the simple act of trying is both exhilarating and comforting.

I tend to shy away from recitation of standard prayers, although some of them are beautiful and comforting. Instead, I find comfort in contemplative prayer. Contemplative prayer is finding a way to block out the world and engage in a dialogue with God through free thought and an open mind. My prayer sessions are often preceded by reading the Bible or reflecting on the words of someone I admire. Buddhists and other religions practice meditation, which at its roots is contemplative prayer.

I have not always been so spiritual. I grew up in the Catholic Church, received all the Sacraments, went to catechism classes, and even served as an altar boy until I grew taller than all the priests and was asked to retire. (In a moment of enlightenment, the Church has redefined this position and opened it up to females. The young people who assist the priest during Mass are now called "servers.") I attended Gannon College, a Catholic institution, and was fairly active in the Church when Eric and Nathan were young.

But three things tested my faith, drove me from the Church, and caused me to question the existence of God. The first was the end of my first marriage despite hours and hours of prayer. The next was the Beast and my perception that it was imposed upon my life as punishment for some unknown sin. Why would a merciful God do that? Finally, representatives of the Catholic Church refused to marry Fran and me because I had been married before. We were, and remain, deeply in love, yet "God's representatives" seemed to be dismissive of this relationship – in effect denying our happiness.

There is a process in the Catholic Church to review a prior Catholic marriage to determine whether it was, in fact, a proper marriage and that the parties were "free" to marry, mentally and spiritually. This process is called "petition for an ecclesiastic declaration of nullity." Most people refer to it as "annulment." At the time Fran and I wanted to marry, the priest we went to for advice described the process of an annulment in such a way that I was left with the impression that I had to disown my sons and "buy my way out" of the marriage. I wanted no part of it.

"Have courage for the great sorrows of life and patience for the small ones; and, when you have laboriously accomplished your daily tasks, go to sleep in peace for God is always awake." **—VICTOR HUGO**

However, as time passed, and the Beast became a more intrusive force in my life, I found myself missing God and desired to re-establish my relationship with Him. Because the Catholic Church had been such a big part of my early life, I naturally gravitated to it to see if there was a place for me among its members. After a while I met Fr. George Vrabel, a true minister of God. Fr. George came to his vocation in a roundabout way. He is a dentist by education but felt that he was "missing something" in his life. He was in his thirties when he trained for the priesthood, but he is an excellent minister because he has experienced life in ways that many priests can't imagine.

After a very long conversation with him, Fr. George told me that "the best thing about God is that He is patient and allows you to come to Him on your own terms. He lets you define how you will relate to Him and the ways you will involve Him in your life. Once you have decided that you want Him in your life, God's love will be there to guide you and for you to draw on as you need it."

I worried that there would be problems between me and the Catholic Church because we disagree on certain issues and ideas that are promulgated in Rome that I believe are not representative of real life in 21st-century America (e.g., the role of women in the ministry). Fr. George put my mind to rest by reminding me that, as long as I came to my positions honestly and after prayerful contemplation, I was in good shape. The door has now opened and I am well along my journey toward making my peace with God and the Catholic Church.

Just accepting the need to have a relationship with God has been as cleansing and comforting as sitting in a warm shower for hours. It has driven my intellectual curiosity to learn more, not just about my faith but also about how God is worshiped by others. I am learning how to read scripture and discern the messages captured in its ancient words. I have also come to know that prayer is not necessarily done in preordained formats but by finding ways to communicate with God by opening my mind and my heart.

This is not an easy task because much of what I learned in my youth as doctrine and fact has changed just as the actual rituals have become much more "user friendly." But the mystery is still there, and I find myself thirsting for more information all the time. Moreover, our parish has become a big part of our lives. I suspect this would probably be true in any faith community if you let it. The social aspects are significant, and it has enabled me to develop some meaningful relationships with people who are eager to have substantive conversations about important matters.

Most importantly, I have found that accepting Jesus Christ as my Lord and Savior has been an unmatchable source of personal refuge and comfort. Through God, I can look for explanations for the unexplainable and find the strength to accept the unacceptable. This kind of understanding, it seems to me, is proportional to the depth of my love of God and of my acceptance of His love for me.

"Church membership does not make you a Christian any more than owning a piano makes you a musician."
—Unknown

The journey to make peace with God is not an easy one and can't be made alone. I need partners to help me see the way and to keep me on the right path. I've already acknowledged the critical role that Fr. George played (he has since moved on to become pastor of another parish), and I continue to receive assistance from others. First and foremost, there is Fran who, because I don't drive, makes it possible to participate in the life of our faith community. I use that term rather than "parish" because parish defines a building and, sometimes, geographic boundaries. "Faith community" acknowledges the fact that it is the people you share your prayers and ideals with that are important.

"Churchgoers are like coals in a fire. When they cling together they keep the flame aglow; when they separate for too long, they die out."
—Reverend Billy Graham

Fr. Larry Martello is the pastor of St. Joseph Parish, the church that Fran and I attend. He is a jovial bear of a man who acts from the perspective that, if you truly want to participate in our faith community, you are welcome. Unlike other priests we have dealt with on our journey, Fr. Larry is a non-judgmental facilitator who works to include rather than exclude people. I especially appreciate the way he, like my dad, tells you where to look for answers rather than providing them. He has become an important friend and confidant in my life.

Among Fr. Larry's skills is the fact that he is an excellent homilist. He regularly turns the mystical parables of the Gospel into meaningful demonstrations of faith that are relevant in today's complex world. As my journey goes forward, I find that the words of his homilies frequently create a desire to read more of the referenced Gospel than the short excerpts presented at Mass. In short, he makes the word of God come alive.

Another partner in my journey is David Miller, a business associate and dear friend who lives in Lubbock, Texas. Each day David sends me a short verse from the Bible via e-mail. The verses remind me who God is and why He is important in my life. These short verses are often a catalyst to read more of the Bible and learn more about God.

One of the very special aspects of our friendship is the fact that David helps me to understand God, His word, and its meaning by presenting it from a different perspective. He describes himself as a "Bible Belt Baptist," but his insights into both scripture and Christianity really defy labeling. I value his insights and appreciate his friendship more than words can say.

Making peace with God, whomever or however you perceive God to exist, is an ongoing process that gives meaning to your life. I'm not sure that the effort will ever be over, and I know it can't be done alone. However, I am calmed by the knowledge that there are times and there are things that can best be handled by giving them over to Christ, who will handle them as God sees fit.

"God does not require that we succeed. He asks only that we try."   **—MOTHER TERESA**

CHAPTER 23

FACE YOUR FEARS SQUARELY

"We have nothing to fear but fear itself."
—PRESIDENT FRANKLIN DELANO ROOSEVELT

FEAR CAN BE EMOTIONALLY paralyzing if you let it. I find that the best way to conquer my fears is to confront them head on. For me, this is a three-step process. First I take the time to research and gain a full understanding of what it is that frightens me. Then I look for ways to modify my life to minimize the impact of the source of my anxiety. Finally, I design and implement a plan to deal with the source of my fears.

As you can imagine, lots of new fears evolve from the Beast's continued efforts to weaken my muscles, increase the problems brought on by fatigue, and subject me to occasional periods of nearly unbearable pain. Similarly, the more you become dependent upon others to assist you with the activities of daily living, the more you wonder what would happen if someone were not around to help you in an emergency. Thus I am sure that you can understand why one of my greatest fears is that, in the process of assisting me, Fran might injure herself, creating quite a pickle for both of us.

My worst fear, however, is that something could happen to Fran that forces me to continue my battle with the Beast without her by my side. I know that God would be there to help me survive, but I also know that life would never be the same and that the word "loneliness" would have new meaning for me.

My analysis of these fears has led me to the inescapable realization that I must not take unnecessary risks and I must plan my days so that I schedule those tasks that require Fran's assistance for times when I'm well rested and able to assist Fran in assisting me. I have also begun to look into what it will take to hire a part-time personal care assistant (PCA) to give Fran a break.

(The only problem with the PCA approach is that I really enjoy those moments when, in the process of lifting and transfers, I get to wrap my arms around my sweetie and give her a big hug – a comforting and very pleasurable experience.)

I have found that the worst kind of fear is irrational fear, anxiety that is based on what-ifs and maybes rather than fact and reality.

During the early struggles of my battle with the Beast, I lived with the fear of being overlooked for professional growth and leadership opportunities because my disability made me appear weak. Rather than face rejection, I would not volunteer for new assignments. Unbeknown to me, the opposite was true. I was at a meeting of Governor Celeste's senior staff where the discussion was about who should take the lead on an important new project. My fear of rejection was allayed when Governor Celeste stood up and slapped the table while saying, "Everyone in this room knows you can handle this, Dave. What's holding you back?" At that moment, I knew that my disability was transparent to the governor and what was important was my abilities.

Caught without a retort, I ended up leading a project that resulted in the passage of major reform legislation that raised the standards for operators of group homes serving people with mental retardation and other developmental disabilities. It was landmark legislation, and my role in making it happen forever washed away my irrational fear that my intellectual abilities would be ignored because of the limitations of my physical disabilities.

There was another positive outcome from this project. The Republicans controlled the State Senate and thus had the ability to block this initiative in order to gain political fodder to use against the governor in his upcoming re-election bid. Even the most optimistic analysts predicted it would take a year or more to move the legislation.

But these pundits did not count on the fact that State Senator (now Congressman) Dave Hobson was chairman of the committee that would handle the legislation. Dave is a man who always puts the welfare of his constituents ahead of political expedience. Senator Hobson met me at his home on Saturday, and by Monday we had a bipartisan plan to address the issue. Dave's leadership combined with my passion created a force that moved the legislation through the Ohio General Assembly in just three months – much to the amazement of everyone.

During the hours we spent working together, we became good friends who realized that we come from different political backgrounds but know that we can work together when it counts. Congressman Hobson is now a powerful committee chairman in Washington but will always make time to talk with me when I'm visiting Capitol Hill. More than a few heads have been turned when they learned that this powerful Republican is a significant financial supporter of this Democrat's city council campaigns.

If I had not faced my irrational fears or if I had said no to the governor when he asked me to take the lead on the group home legislation project, I would have missed the chance to work and become friends with Congressman Hobson.

Facing your fears squarely almost always leads to positive outcomes and can be the catalyst for learning new skills and building new, important relationships.

CHAPTER 24

THE BATTLE RAGES ON

"There are only two ways to live your life. One is to live as if nothing were a miracle. The other is to live as if everything is a miracle." **—ALBERT EINSTEIN**

MY WAR WITH THE BEAST continues. I like to think that I have prevailed in many of the battles and found ways to mitigate the impact of its occasional victories. Despite the obvious negatives, my life goes on, and I am acutely aware that the Beast will be an ever-present force in it. I know that there are great challenges ahead, but I choose to see them as great opportunities as well.

"There are no great men; only great challenges which ordinary men must meet and overcome."
—ADMIRAL BULL HALSEY

As the writing of this book nears conclusion, I am simultaneously in the midst of another major life change, courtesy of the Beast.

It has become clear to both me and my employer that my position requires the kind of full-time energy and attention I can no longer give it: 60-hour work weeks, frequent and spontaneous travel, and periods of intense pressure to make quick decisions that have the potential to have a profound impact on thousands of people. So, a replacement has been found, and I have retired from my position as Director of Government Relations. Mal Mixon and the leadership of Invacare have promised to continue to find meaningful ways for me to remain part of the Invacare team – to begin with, in a consulting role on political and legislative strategy.

As if accepting early retirement from Invacare was not

enough of a blow, I lost my bid for reelection to the Amherst City Council just as the preparations to send this book to the printer were nearing completion. I lost by five votes out of over 4000 cast – remember that the next time you think that your vote doesn't count! Even I thought I would be more disappointed by the election results than I was. Don't get me wrong. I love public service and will continue to be involved in our community in any way I can. But public service is not linked to holding elected office.

After enduring the tedious process of a recount, I found myself saying, "God must have a different plan for me." I may run again in two years, but for now, I am quite fulfilled playing a more active role in my church, serving the city as its ADA compliance officer and in other roles, and immersing myself further in the activities of the Amherst Historical Society. Once again, I am reminded, *as one door closes another opens.*

The most frightening aspect of this particular transition is that it means leaving the security of a regular paycheck and its associated benefit plan for all the chaos and idiosyncrasies of relying on a long-term disability plan and, possibly, Social Security for my income. Worse, Medicare will eventually become my primary source of health insurance. I have spent the last 25 years of my life studying and working to reform the Medicare program, and I know too much about it to be confident that it will adequately cover my complex health care needs.

Nonetheless, I am confident that Fran and I will work our way through this challenging new environment and look forward to having more time to spend together. I also see this new setback as a setup for yet another comeback!

My two biggest challenges are learning to make smart decisions on how to use my limited time and energy and accepting the fact that I must frequently ask for help.

Asking for help is not as easy as it seems. Most people would tell you that I am as stubborn as a mule and have an independent streak a mile wide. These traits are in direct conflict with the limitations the Beast challenges me with every day. As I have said, most days I can't even dress or undress myself without Fran's help. Someone has to drive me whenever I must go a distance of more than four miles (about as far as I can confidently venture in my power chair) or if the weather is bad. There are days when I need help eating. But people are more understanding than you would expect and much more willing to help than you would believe.

I am truly blessed by the fact that I do not have to face the future alone. I have Fran, my family, and my friends to help me. I am realizing what Alexander Graham Bell meant about *one door closing as another door opens.*

John "Shorty" Dietrich is the president of our city council, and he and his wife, Barb, are an important part of our "extended family." Shorty retired by choice recently after selling a very successful contracting business. He shares my interest in local politics and history. He also knows more about the Beast than most of my friends because his first wife had MS and died from complications associated with the disease.

> **"Associate yourself with men of good quality if you esteem your own reputation. It is far better to be alone than in bad company."**
> **—President George Washington**

Shorty has lived in Amherst all his life and has a tremendous understanding of what makes the community tick. He shares that knowledge with me and involves me in key discussions about issues important to our town. Shorty has also found ways to get me involved in the Amherst Historical Society (of which he is president) in very meaningful ways. He understands the limitations imposed by the Beast and goes out of his way to help Fran and me deal with the obstacles it places in our paths. For example, because I can't drive, he helps out so much with my transportation that he and Fran have keys to each other's vehicles. If I need to be at a meeting, he drives our van and Fran can get around in his car. The only downside to this arrangement is that it has generated a little small town gossip in which we all find great humor.

Over time, Shorty has been able to anticipate and assist with the little things that can make my life easier and less frustrating. Without speaking, he helps set things up when we are eating together. For example, I now must use special utensils and a cup with an open handle, and I need a plate guard because I can't always control my "push stroke" to get my food onto the fork or spoon. I sometimes drop things and Shorty just picks them up without any fanfare. He knows the accessible entrances to every building in town and just goes to them automatically. His every action accommodates my disability in a seamless and very comfortable manner. As such, he has engendered a level of trust that can't be quantified. Through his sensitivity and actions, he has helped make my disabilities transparent to many people.

> **"The passage of time reveals the immutable truth that it is the deeds of man that define him, not the words he has spoken no matter how high-sounding they may be."** —SIR WINSTON CHURCHILL

The truth of Churchill's words is exemplified by people like Shorty, Clark Bruner (whom I mentioned earlier), and my brother Jim. They are, in every sense of the words, true friends. I gain strength from their very presence in my life.

> **"It is better to grasp the universe as it really is than to persist in delusion, however satisfying and reassuring."** —CARL SAGAN

Thanks to people like Fran, my extended family, and

dozens of good friends, my life will always be rich. There will always be something new to learn, a new topic of conversation, or a new question to research. No matter what new symptoms the Beast may impose upon my body, there is a lot to look forward to.

"The saddest thing about life right now is that science gathers knowledge faster than society gathers wisdom." —Sir Isaac Asimov

I am aware that the nature of my Beast is such that no one can predict what new challenges lie ahead. When I think about them, I get frightened; so I try to ignore that aspect of it and try to live in the moment. If and when things change, I'll try my hardest to deal with it.

I am often asked if I ever consider giving up or if I ever feel overwhelmed by the Beast and what it may impose upon my life as time passes.

There are days when the pain or fatigue is so intense that I wonder, just for a moment, if it is worth all the effort to continue. But before I can dwell on the negative for very long, I am inevitably reminded of a task that must be finished, things that I have not yet had the opportunity to say to Fran or Eric or Nathan and, now, Jaxson, or a request for help from a friend or neighbor. The idea of giving up is quickly washed away by the knowledge that there is so much left to do in my life.

"Death is a distant rumor to the young." —Andy Rooney

Fran and I work hard at staying young, or at least young at heart. We involve ourselves in activities and organizations that include people of all age groups who dwell on the present and the possible and don't discuss what they are going to do in their "golden years." The lives of our sons, daughters-in-law, and now our grandson are constant reminders of what it is like to have your whole life in front of you and that is how we think.

Nonetheless, I do have a few fears. Like most Americans, I fear that I may not have done enough to ensure our financial security as Fran and I move inexorably closer to our golden years. I am acutely aware of how complex and costly my health care needs are, and I fear that my care will be compromised by our nation's inability to insure adequate health care for all its citizens. I also fear that all the extra things that Fran does to make my life possible will have a negative impact on her health and longevity.

Nonetheless, I look forward to the years ahead, knowing that the Beast will most likely impose its will on me in ways that I would rather avoid. While I don't know what I'll be doing, I am confident that the God of my heart has a plan for me, and I find great comfort in that fact. No matter what happens, I am equally confident that my prayers will be answered, and when I close my eyes that last time, I will know that I did my best to make a difference during my time on this earth.

AFTERWORD

WRITING THIS BOOK has been a tremendous experience. It has forced me to face many demons and make my peace with them. I have had to reflect on periods of my life as well as specific incidents that I would rather forget. But in the process, I have learned a lot about myself – my strengths, my weaknesses, and the way I handle challenges.

The conclusion of this effort comes at a time of great uncertainty and new challenges resulting from my battle with the Beast. I know that I will survive and go on to accomplish many things before my God calls me home. I go forward knowing that my work is not yet completed and whatever the tasks are that lie before me, I can and will complete them.

Now it is time to leave you to deal with the Beasts in your lives. If I have succeeded, you have found some answers on the pages of this book that will help you face your challenges. Always remember that regardless of the form of your particular Beast or the size of the challenges that will accentuate your lives, you can prevail.

To be honest, I have struggled to find the last words I wanted to share with the readers of this book. My friend Max Cleland, in true Southern fashion, provided me with some words that really sum up my life. The author is unknown, and the words are not recorded in history as much as they are repeated in legend. The story is that these were the last words of a Confederate soldier who wrote them as he lay dying in a Union field hospital near the end of the Civil War or, as the people of the South refer to it, the War Between the States. I will close this book by sharing them with you. They aptly describe my life to date.

I asked God for strength that I might achieve,
I was made weak, that I might learn humbly to obey.

I asked for health, that I might do greater things,
I was given infirmity that I might do better things.

I asked for riches that I might be happy,
I was given poverty that I might be wise.

I asked for power, that I might have the praise of men,
I was given weakness that I might feel the need of God.

I asked for all things, that I might enjoy life,
I was given life that I might enjoy all things.
I got nothing that I asked for, but everything I had hoped for.
Almost despite myself, my unspoken prayers were answered.

I am among all men, most richly blessed.